final events on planet earth

Final Events on Planet Earth

By Norman Gulley

Southern Publishing Association, Nashville, Tennessee

Copyright © 1977 by
Southern Publishing Association

This book was
Edited by Gerald Wheeler
Designed by Mark O'Connor
Cover photo by Loren McIntye

Type set: 11/13 Century Schoolbook

Printed in U.S.A.

Library of Congress Cataloging in Publication Data
Gulley, Norman R
    Final events on planet earth.

    1. Eschatology. I. Title.
BT821.2.G84   236   77-24206
ISBN 0-8127-0144-5

CONTENTS

Chapter 1

Is the World
Out of Control?

Dr. Edmund Leach, provost of King's College, Cambridge University, spoke of a "runaway world" in the Reith lectures over the British Broadcasting Corporation. Commenting later Principal Michael Green, of St. John's Hall, Nottingham, noted that the lectures were "to draw attention to the fact that the world seems to be getting out of the control of leading scientists and politicians." Even Christians have wondered. J. B. Phillips commented, "Many Christians suffer today, more perhaps than in any preceding age, from a sense that the world is out of control."[1]

A plethora of problems seems to support the conclusion. The economy has run awry since oil prices skyrocketed. One observer warns, "Most of the countries of the western world in general are seriously ill."[2] Even America, the land of plenty, has experienced a record slump. Add to the problem the world's appalling food shortage, with forty million dead from starvation in one recent year and a birth rate approaching one hundred million a year—no wonder an agronomist predicted, "We may be seeing the beginning of the end of our civilization."[3]

Crime statistics leap higher, and international terrorism reaches epidemic proportions. A pollution of horror floods the market. A recent brochure of Macmillan's Audio Brandon lists two hundred films on giant leeches, brain eaters, devil worshipers, blood beasts, screaming skulls, and vampire lovers. In our so-called post-Christian era, when the occult mushrooms and many Christian churches have lost their grip, Pope Paul VI admitted on the eve of the fourth world synod of bishops, "The church seems destined to die."

Mankind seems destined to complete annihilation. Philosophies of nihilism and despair such as those of Sartre and Nietzsche seem increasingly valid. What has happened to Alexander Pope's dictum: "Hope springs eternal in the human breast"? Can man really hope anymore? Can it spring from within when surrounded by so much gloom?

I suggest that an entirely new dimension is necessary, a looking beyond to another and better world. It is not sufficient to say as Artis Whitman did in the *Reader's Digest* of December, 1974*, "Hope is a goal in itself." For as a child is born from a mother, so hope arises from a sure goal. It is never a goal in itself, even as a baby cannot be his own mother. The lack of a goal, a purpose, a sense of direction, leads many to believe that our world is out of control and hurtling to destruction.

But why no goal? We could ask the question in another way. Why has Christianity been turned upside down in our century when it turned the

---

* Asian edition, p. 93, from article "That Vital Spark—Hope."

FINAL EVENTS ON PLANET EARTH

world upside down in the first century? Why do many refer to our age as the post-Christian era? Why are churches so ineffective?

The first-century church made an impact, its presence felt, because it had a goal. It looked beyond the passing problems of the present world to the permanent peace of the one to come. The trouble nowadays is that many Christians have settled down in the Egypt of today's existence, forgetting that they have a heavenly Canaan to enter. They haven't ceased to help in social problems, but they have no "other-world" good news to proclaim. It is such news—such light from beyond the gloom—that would make all the difference. J. B. Phillips well stated, "In our modern preoccupation with Christian social justice and the relevance of the Christian faith to all human problems, we tend to forget the heaven to which we are bound." [4]

Only an unshakable faith in a better world to come will give Christians a message of hope to endure the present one. Without it Christianity will always remain ineffective. "It is since Christians have ceased to think of the other world that they have become so ineffective in this," cried out C. S. Lewis. "Aim at Heaven and you will get earth 'thrown in': aim at earth and you will get neither." [5]

Many today feel like Job—time trudges on "day after hopeless day" (Job 7:6, TLB). But it doesn't have to be so. David declared, "On thee, O Lord, I fix my hope" (Psalm 38:15, NEB). Solomon said, "I will hope in him" (Lamentations 3:24, RSV). Jeremiah affirmed, "Thou art my hope" (Jeremiah

IS THE WORLD OUT OF CONTROL?

17:17, KJV), and Paul pointed to "Jesus Christ, which is our hope" (1 Timothy 1:1, KJV). He is the ultimate goal of hope. Hope has its root and ground in a Person and not merely in a place. "Happy is he . . . whose hope is in the Lord his God" (Psalm 146:5, KJV).

Hope's supreme goal, the source from which it really springs eternal, is not in man, but in the "God of hope," who is eternal. It is not by working it up from within but "by the power of the Holy Spirit [that] you may abound in hope" (Romans 15:13, RSV). Even though man's efforts have brought him into the mess in which he finds himself, he still thinks that through his own efforts he can find a way out. But "those who forget God have no hope" (Job 8:13, TLB). Christians must tell the world, as Dr. John Baillie did, that "the transference of attention from self to God is the secret of both self-conquest and hope."[6]

Modern man desperately needs to look away from the present world to the one to come. Even more important, he needs to look away from self to Christ. Hope has its root and ground in Him alone. As E. Stanley Jones put it, Jesus Christ is "God's total answer to man's total need."[7] Phillips Brooks was right when he wrote of Bethlehem, "The hopes and fears of all the years/Are met in thee tonight."

Hope has appeared in the form of Jesus Christ, God's Son. He shattered the kingdom of Satan. His victorious cry on the cross, "It is finished," forever settled the sin problem. He will rescue man. The second return of Christ is certain, for it is the inevitable conclusion of Calvary's triumph. He died here in our world for us that we might live

FINAL EVENTS ON PLANET EARTH

in the better world with Him.

"The Lord himself will descend from heaven with a cry of command, with the archangel's call, and with the sound of the trumpet of God. And the dead in Christ will rise first; then we who are alive, who are left, shall be caught up together with them in the clouds to meet the Lord in the air; and so we shall always be with the Lord. Therefore comfort one another with these words" (1 Thessalonians 4:16-18, RSV).

Current crises do not surprise Jesus Christ; He predicted them: famines (Matthew 24:7); social unrest (Matthew 24:6); lack of faith in Him (Luke 18:8)—to name a few. Knowledge that God foresaw such conditions inspires confidence that He really is in control. Too many of us forget the fact. Seeing the surrounding problems closing in on us, we let ourselves get cut off from the only Being who can inspire hope, and then we have no one to turn to. We feel utterly alone, having forgotten that faith in God would make all the difference, for such "faith gives substance to our hopes" (Hebrews 11:1, NEB). But if you keep your focus on the victorious, living, coming King, you will have "a living hope" indeed (1 Peter 1:3, RSV).

The ship plowed through the Atlantic, making good time. England lay far behind; Canada, days away. But a heavy fog moved in and enveloped the ship. With visibility nil and radar not yet invented, the vessel slowed to a crawl. A passenger, George Müller by name, walked along the deck, hands in pockets, and eyed the fog. He needed to be at a meeting in just three days.

Müller thought of his many decades of an-

IS THE WORLD OUT OF CONTROL?

swered prayer. Through prayer alone God had given him five orphanages, housing nearly ten thousand orphans. Not once had he asked others for money. God knew his needs and led them to send adequate funds for his large family.

Slowly Müller climbed to where the captain stood on the bridge. "Captain, I need to be in port in just three days. I have an appointment to meet." He paused to catch his breath. "I have never broken an appointment in my life, and I believe that God will get me there."

The captain shuffled his feet, wiped his tired eyes, and looked at the strange man. "I'd like to help you, Mr. Müller, but it's impossible. Don't you see this bad fog?"

Gazing into the captain's strained face, Müller replied, "Sir, I do not see the fog but the God who controls the fog. Come with me, captain; let us pray to Him. Never has He failed to answer my prayers." The captain felt strangely drawn to his passenger, and before he knew it, found himself kneeling with Müller in a quiet room below. "Father," Müller prayed briefly, "You know I need to be at a meeting by Sunday. I know that You can take care of this fog. Thank You for doing so. Amen."

Gently Müller laid his hand on the captain's shoulder. "Captain, get up, open the door, and you'll see that the fog has gone."

"How could it be?" the officer thought. But he arose, swung the door open—and the fog had vanished. Müller kept his appointment.

God does not usually choose to answer prayers so dramatically. He knows best. The real point of

FINAL EVENTS ON PLANET EARTH

the story is what George Müller focused on. Refusing to allow surrounding circumstances to get him down, he looked beyond them to God. He trusted in a God who is in control. You can do the same.

---

[1]J. B. Phillips, *Making Men Whole* (New York: The Macmillan Company, 1953), p. 7.

[2]*Newsweek,* September 30, 1974, p. 63.

[3]*Newsweek,* November 11, 1974, p. 56.

[4]Phillips, *op. cit.*, pp. 8, 9.

[5]C. S. Lewis, *Mere Christianity* (London: Fontana Books, Collins, 1955), p. 116.

[6]John Baillie, *And the Life Everlasting* (Alesbury and Slough: Wyvern Books, Oxford University Press, 1961), p. 124.

[7]E. Stanley Jones, *The Word Became Flesh* (New York: Abingdon Press, 1963), p. 382.

IS THE WORLD OUT OF CONTROL?

Chapter 2

Is Your God Too Small?

Albert Schweitzer claimed that Jesus was a failure! "There is silence all around. The Baptist appears, and cries: 'Repent, for the Kingdom of Heaven is at hand.' Soon after that comes Jesus, and in the knowledge that He is the coming Son of Man lays hold of the wheel of the world to set it moving on that last revolution which is to bring all ordinary history to a close. It refuses to turn, and He throws Himself upon it. Then it does turn; and crushes Him. Instead of bringing in the eschatological conditions, He has destroyed them. The wheel rolls onward, and the mangled body of the one immeasurably great Man, who was strong enough to think of Himself as the spiritual ruler of mankind and to bend history to His purpose, is hanging upon it still. That is His victory and His reign."[1]

Here is a tragic picture of God—unable to control circumstances—helplessly trapped in them. Schweitzer's God was too small.

In thunder tones come the words of Richard Le Gallienne,

"Loud mockers in the roaring street
    Say Christ is crucified again:

> Twice pierced His gospel-bearing feet,
> Twice broken His great heart in vain.

> "I hear, and to myself I smile,
> For Christ talks with me all the while."[2]

The New Testament throbs with the vibrant good news. The resurrection has shattered human history in a great creative act as stupendous as that in the beginning. The startling declaration jumps out from every sermon proclaimed by the early church—"He is risen!" "He is risen!" Like a mighty wave it sweeps over the sea of time, taking all other things in its wake. Gone is the old. Broken into human history is the new. The resurrection makes the decisive difference.

No wonder J. B. Phillips could say, "A man may find difficulty in writing a poem, but if he cries, 'Oh, William Shakespeare, help me!' nothing whatever happens. A man may be terribly afraid, but if he cries, 'Oh, Horatio Nelson, help me!' there is no sort of reply. But if he is at the end of his moral resources or cannot by effort of will muster up sufficient positive love and goodness and he cries, 'Oh, Christ, help me!' something happens at once. The sense of spiritual reinforcement, of drawing spiritual vitality from a living source, is so marked that Christians cannot help being convinced that their Hero is far more than an outstanding figure of the past."[3]

One hot Easter Sunday, three hours' drive north of Manila, I watched a forty-year-old bearded Filipino fisherman nailed to a cross. His picture of God was of one that you could bargain

FINAL EVENTS ON PLANET EARTH

with, one who would help you if you would help yourself. He promised to have himself nailed to a cross five times, in five consecutive years, for the healing of his baby daughter. As I looked up to the agony of his face as he hung from the wood, I wanted to shout out, "He is risen, He has already died, there is no need for another cross. Come down, you are free." His God was too small.

But was John Calvin any better? His God supposedly made an eternal decree, choosing to save some and to damn others. Here is a partial God, one who has favorites. Calvin's God was too small. Friedrich Schleiermacher in the nineteenth century reduced God to an inner feeling of dependence within man. Little better is Tillich's view that God is the ground of all being. Whether God is someone within man or is something upon which all life is contingent, we still have too small a God. Perhaps the "death of God" theologians took some of such thinking to a logical conclusion when, like Schweitzer, they believed God to be dead today. This theology of the 1960's exposed the "dead-end bankruptcy" of a God who is less than the Biblical revelation.

The examples above are but a few of the many that we could cite. How about your God? Is He too small? What picture of Him do you have, particularly as you consider the resurrected Christ standing before His Father in the heavenly sanctuary?

"Ah," says a friend, "you mean to say you believe in the intercession of Jesus before His Father? Does the Father need to have someone plead with Him? That isn't any better than the activity of the saints conceived of by Catholics. You just believe in Christ's intercession because He was human and therefore understands us more. His Father never became a man, and therefore the Son must inform Him of the human misery that He never experienced first hand Himself. If it weren't for Christ's intercession, we would have no hope." Is this your picture of God?

How would you answer such questions? Is Jesus the God-man pleading before His Father because He has more empathy with man than the Father has? No, a thousand times no! The Bible rules out such a conclusion. "For God [the Father] so loved the world, that he gave his only begotten Son, that whosoever believeth in him should not perish, but have everlasting life" (John 3:16, KJV).

Let the words of Jesus ring out loud and clear. "At that day ye shall ask in my name: and I say not unto you, that I will pray the Father for you: for the Father himself loveth you" (John 16:26, 27, KJV). In other words: "It is not necessary for Me to pray or intercede before the Father for you, for He already loves you. My intercession has nothing to do with changing Him. There is an utterly different motive involved." And what is it?

Heaven's courtroom finds God on trial more than man—which comes as a surprise to many. We find ourselves in a great conflict between Christ and Satan. Satan has charged God with making a law too high for anyone to keep. Therefore he alleges that God is unjust. The fact that Satan, his angels, and all men have fallen short of His law's standard he offers as evidence of divine injustice.

FINAL EVENTS ON PLANET EARTH

It is one reason Jesus came to live as a man. He kept that law as a man, with no advantage over us. When on the cross He cried, "It is finished," He not only died to save us, but He completed a perfect life to forever answer Satan's charge. But why then the investigative judgment now? And why two other judgments to come?

Our God is big! He doesn't just prove but overproves, to the complete and utter satisfaction of all involved. It is His character to supply abundantly. We find that fact throughout nature. Many kinds of fruit contain large amounts of seeds. Likewise, God gives more than ample evidence to show what He really is like. Look at it this way. In the present assize Jesus stands in as your Advocate, answering Satan's false charges against you. The devil knows all the sins you have committed and wants to rob you of heaven. Demon that he is, he seeks to drag every last human to degradation and destruction with himself. But great as God is, He will not let Satan do it. Christ has lived and died for men, and in the judgment He pleads His sacrifice in their behalf. He has a right to claim them as His own because He bought them back.

Zechariah 3 clearly gives us the picture. Michael answers the adversary in behalf of Joshua. The Father doesn't need the intercession, but He merely watches over all the proceedings with the same empathy His Son has for the fallen race. It would be just as easy for the Father to take the place of the Son and make the same compassionate appeal. But Jesus was the one who died for men, and therefore it is logical that He plead for

IS YOUR GOD TOO SMALL?

those for whom He gave His own life.

Did you ever stop to think why God convenes three judgments—the present judgment, the judgment during the thousand years, and the judgment at the close of the millennium? Why so many? It's the same reason why He conducts any at all—God wants everyone to be fully satisfied with His justice. He convenes the several sessions for the sake of His creatures, that they may know the truth about Him. The present judgment finds the onlooking universe given all the facts on why His people can be saved. During the millennium the redeemed, together with the rest of intelligent creation, will see why the majority of humans were lost. But before the destruction of the lost, after the millennium, God allows every human who has ever existed to live once more. All of God's creatures—alive at the same time—will look into the records of those who will be lost. Even Satan and his angels, as well as all the condemned human rebels, will fall to their knees in admission of God's utter justice. At that moment no person will have one lingering doubt as to who has been right in the struggle between good and evil. They will see Satan utterly exposed and Jesus Christ completely exonerated.

In the light of the three judgments, our God is great—He is in control!

---

[1] Albert Schweitzer, *The Quest of the Historical Jesus* (London: Adam and Charles Black, 1963), p. 368, 369.

[2] Richard Le Gallienne, "The Second Crucifixion," quoted in James S. Stewart, *A Faith to Proclaim* (New York: Charles Scribner's Sons, 1953), p. 116.

[3] J. B. Phillips, *Your God Is Too Small* (New York: The Macmillan Company, 1969), p. 127.

FINAL EVENTS ON PLANET EARTH

Chapter 3

What Is the
Sign of the End?*

dying out

"Matthew 24 is as moribund as *Life* magazine! Give us something contemporary. The sun, moon, and stars did their thing before my grandparents were born. Besides, all the wars, famines, and false christs mentioned in the chapter—they have plagued people through the centuries. What's new under the sun anyway? Where, indeed, is the promise of His coming? How do you know when the end will come? Is it near or far? Give us *the* sign of the end."

"Remember 1948?" shouts one in reply. "That's the date—the real sign—something you can hang on. Israel returned to Palestine in 1948. She heralds the imminent end." Hal Lindsey's book *The Late Great Planet Earth,* sold by the millions, says Israel has "great significance as a sign of the time."[1] And a staggering number of Christians agree. But why?

Most Christians believe Israel is the last great evidence of Christ's second coming because the Jews, they say, must reoccupy Palestine before

---

*For some ideas in this chapter, I am indebted to Dr. Hans LaRondelle of Andrews University and to the books of Pastor L. F. Were.

Jesus can return to earth. Numerous texts quoted from Old Testament prophets seem to substantiate their claim. But more careful study reveals that the Bible never speaks of a physical migration to Palestine preceding a spiritual return to God.

God did not call Abraham, the father of the Jews, out of Ur and lead him to Palestine in order to bring him to Himself. Abraham first believed in God, and therefore God called him. Later the summons to leave Egyptian slavery came to Jews who had already experienced the Passover. Forty years after the Exodus, only the faithful spies, Joshua and Caleb, finally entered the land. The faithless of their generation perished in the desert.

Centuries passed. The Jews now in Babylonian captivity heard a new plea to return. But only those committed to God responded—the others stayed behind in Babylon.

Thus the Bible clearly indicates that God calls a person, or people, to Himself before taking them to a place. The same principle must apply for any further supposed modern-day fulfillment of prophecy. But modern Israel has occupied Palestine before accepting God and His Son Jesus. Christians who find in the modern state of Israel a sign of the end fail to see its disparity with the Biblical data. Further, they even look for a future acceptance of God by the Jews, and that leads them to another wild claim.

They argue that the future contains a seven-year period initiated by a secret rapture, or taking, of all living Christians to heaven. Suddenly Christian pilots and bus and train drivers will disappear, abandoning helpless passengers to become crash

FINAL EVENTS ON PLANET EARTH

victims. The upheaval will be unprecedented. The utter chaos resulting from such a disappearance will result in the greatest crime ever pulled off by a body of people. And yet they believe that it is really God who will do it. What a distorted view of God!

Such teaching supposedly has its basis in 1 Thessalonians 4:16-18. But even a cursory view of the passage leads one to a different conclusion. It speaks of the resounding trump of God to awaken all the righteous dead. Imagine the shout of triumph of the redeemed at their deliverance and the exclamations of joy as loved ones reunite. The tumultuous welcome given to the ascending redeemed by their guardian angels and the hosts of heaven who have long waited for the moment has to make it the noisest passage in the Bible—thus, far from a secret rapture.

The seven-year period to convert the Jews is allegedly the seventieth week of Daniel 9:24. But wait a minute. The sixty-ninth week ended with Christ (Daniel 9:25), or nearly two thousand years ago. Who ever heard of skipping a couple of millennia just to force a Bible passage to say what you want it to say?

Dispensationalism, which considers the modern state of Israel to represent the great final sign of Christ's imminent return, began with John Nelson Darby of Great Britain in the early nineteenth century. It is a variety of futurism which goes back to the Jesuit priest Ribera, who about 1590 published a commentary on Revelation.

Jumping the Atlantic, pushing across the United States, dispensationalism broke into every

WHAT IS THE SIGN OF THE END?

major church. Rapidly gaining popularity, boosted and solidified by its 1909 Scofield Reference Bible, it became seemingly impregnable and unmovable with the creation of Israel in 1948.

The doctrine cunningly counterfeits the Seventh-day Adventist message. Ours summons people out of Babylon to join spiritual Israel preparing to meet Christ in a literal advent. Dispensationalists look the other way—concentrating on a calling out from nations to form a literal Israel and focus on a spiritual advent of Christ in the secret rapture. The two views diametrically oppose each other. If one accepts dispensationalism, he seems almost impossible to reach with Adventism. A large number of Christians are in this group. At the 1971 conference on prophecy in Jerusalem, all but one of the speakers thought Israel's presence in Palestine fulfilled Old Testament prophecy.

Israel stood divided, half on the slopes of Mt. Gerizim and half under the shadow of Mt. Ebal. Ahead lay the long-looked-for Promised Land, behind stretched the almost endless desert. Joshua led in the solemn recital of God's covenant promises, which included cursings as well as blessings—cursings overlooked by dispensationalists.

The record appears in Deuteronomy 28. A remarkable unveiling of Israel's future comes to view. It hides nothing. Obey and stay—or disobey and disperse: "And the Lord will scatter you among all peoples, from one end of the earth to the other" (Deuteronomy 28:64, RSV). And scattered they were—by the Assyrians, Babylonians, and Romans.

FINAL EVENTS ON PLANET EARTH

Deuteronomy 30 contains promises of return. God will gather Israel from "all the nations" (verse 1). If you, Israel, will "return unto the Lord" with all your hearts, "then the Lord thy God . . . will return and gather thee from all the nations . . . into the land which thy fathers possessed" (verses 2-5, KJV). The Old Testament often repeats the promise (see Jeremiah 30:3; 31:8-14; Ezekiel 39:25-28; Amos 9:11-15).

The Bible compares the gathering to a second exodus (Isaiah 11:11-15), but from all nations rather than just one. However, dispensationalists claim that Jews returned from exile from only one nation—Babylon—and therefore 1948 must be the second gathering from all nations. But Isaiah 11:15 calls the exodus from Egypt the first, and thus the trek back from Babylon would be the second. Moreover, the second assembling of the Jews came not just from Babylon but from many nations, as the Hebrew captives had been sold to international merchants (see Joel 3:2-6).

God rejected the Jews as a nation (Matthew 23:38) because they chose to spurn Him (John 19:14-16). But eventually one Israelite did what they did not—Jesus remained true to the covenant. Old Testament history moves toward this one Israelite, and from Him arises ultimate victory in the New Testament. Israel is now the church, and the heavenly temple has superseded the earthly. God's faithful remnant live on in a new form.

The early church interpreted the Old Testament promises to spiritual Israel. One example appears in the Jerusalem Council called because of controversy over Gentile admissions to the

WHAT IS THE SIGN OF THE END?

church. James summed up Peter's report in Acts 15:13-16, " 'Brethren, listen to me, Symeon has related how God first visited the Gentiles, to take out of them a people for his name. And with this the words of the prophets agree, as it is written, "After this I will return, and I will rebuild the dwelling of David, which has fallen; I will rebuild its ruins, and I will set it up" ' " (RSV).

The apostle referred to Amos 9:11. The context speaks of scattering Israel to the nations (verse 9), followed by a gathering and restoration (verses 11-15). James used the Old Testament gathering promise in its post-Calvary New Testament fulfillment—as an assembling—not to a nation—but of Gentiles into the church, into spiritual Israel.

In the same way the promise to make Israel a holy nation, a royal priesthood, given in Exodus 19:5, 6, Peter applies to spiritual Israel (1 Peter 2:9), and John sees it finding ultimate fulfillment in the new earth after the millennium (Revelation 5:10). Many prophecies which only had partial fulfillment in the Old Testament gain fuller unfolding in the Christian era, but we still look for total completion in the new heavens and new earth.

The Bible is not secular history but salvation history. It reveals the conflict between Christ and Satan. Scripture interests itself in Israel, not as a nation, but as God's people. Other countries come into the picture only as they relate to God's chosen ones. In the Old Testament the prophets speak of Babylon as the great enemy of Israel. After the cross the literal becomes spiritual—the nation becomes a church, and physical Babylon transforms into spiritual Babylon.

FINAL EVENTS ON PLANET EARTH

Reaching out, the apostles added Gentiles and Jews to the new form of Israel, the church. During the Dark Ages Babylon was the Catholic system. Luther broke away from it with a call to come out. The exodus out of Catholicism into Protestantism represented a further development of spiritual Israel.

A few generations after the death of Luther and Calvin, Protestantism deteriorated, as had the early church. Degeneration set in so that by the nineteenth century another summons to leave Babylon to join Israel became necessary. God moved upon William Miller to give the invitation. No secret-rapture whim grasped him by the neck. Rather, "The Lord is coming" was his cry. He preached a literal advent and no nonsense about Israel. In fact he said, "There is not a text, promise, or prophecy, written or given of God" to suggest that the Lord would reestablish Israel in Palestine.[2]

The Seventh-day Adventist Church has as its commission to give "the three angels' messages" to the world. They urge man to leave spiritual Babylon and to enter spiritual Israel in order to prepare for the literal coming of Jesus (Revelation 14:6-20). Revelation 18 tells of a final cry to flee Babylon into Israel.

Since Christ's day we have seen a gathering into spiritual Israel, a repeated coming out of Babylonian captivity. It is taking place all over the world today as a preparation for Christ's physical advent. Seen in this context, it has always been to a Person and never just to a place. The Messianic promises and the gathering prophecies intertwine as one. The Lord always was interested

WHAT IS THE SIGN OF THE END?

in being a God to His people. Such a relationship lies at the heart of the covenant (Deuteronomy 29:13). The place of residence, Palestine, was immaterial. Thus the New Testament speaks in terms of Abraham's looking for a city whose builder and maker is God—a heavenly and not just an earthly country (Hebrews 11:10). The modern state of Israel is a puny sign when viewed in the light of Biblical facts.

Israel is not the sign of the end—and yet it is. Spiritual Israel, now forming from a worldwide exodus out of spiritual Babylon, constitutes *the* sign of the end. Matthew 24:14 speaks of the gospel's going to all the world—then shall the end come. Never before has the gathering been so universal as today. Its climax is imminent. It speaks of a God in control.

---

[1] Hal Lindsey, *The Late Great Planet Earth* (Grand Rapids, Michigan: Zondervan Publishing House, 1970), p. 50.

[2] See *A Symposium on Biblical Hermeneutics,* ed. G. M. Hyde (Washington, D.C.: Review and Herald Publishing Association, 1974), p. 116.

FINAL EVENTS ON PLANET EARTH

Chapter 4

Are You Weak?

On Saturday, September 4, 1869, Hudson Taylor arrived at his tiny, crowded home in Chinkiang, China, after a mission itinerary. "It's been a long, hot summer," he sighed. He kissed his wife and children, greeted the Chinese teachers and other missionaries, and as if driven by some inner searching, went to his study. Now he wanted some peace. Although he had prayed, agonized, fasted, made resolutions, read the Bible even more, still his inner self seemed in turmoil, and he felt himself a great sinner and failure. Picking up a stack of correspondence that had accumulated during his absence, he idly turned the envelopes. Why couldn't he get relief?

"John McCarthy," he read on the envelope. His pulse quickened, and he hastily tore open the envelope. Why, it was from the young Irishman he had just left in Hangchow. He recalled well John's quick temper and how the man desired to overcome it. The letter was long.

"I see," wrote McCarthy, "as if the first glimmer of the dawn of a glorious day has arisen upon me. . . . I seem to have sipped only of that which can fully satisfy."

"What's he found?" Taylor, hardly able to read fast enough, asked himself. The letter continued: "To let my loving Saviour work in me His will, . . . abiding, not striving or struggling. . . . Not a striving to have faith or to increase our faith, but a looking at the faithful one seems all we need."

"Looking at the faithful one." Taylor stared long out the window as he thought of his Saviour, and a wave of peace, joy, and contentment flowed through his whole being. With new joy in his heart he called the household together and read McCarthy's letter to them, exclaiming, "I am one with Christ; I am part of Him. Each of us is a limb of His body, a branch of the vine."

Centuries before, Jesus Christ had stated, "I am the vine, ye are the branches: he that abideth in me, and I in him, the same bringeth forth much fruit: for without me ye can do nothing" (John 15:5, KJV). McCarthy and Taylor now saw that spiritual victory comes through abiding rather than through fighting, that obedience comes not through trying harder but through trusting more. For obedience is the result of an intimate relationship with Jesus Christ.

"Ah, but wait a minute!" calls a work addict. "Isn't there something I have to do before Christ can accept me in order for me to abide in Him? After all, Taylor and McCarthy served as missionaries."

Back comes the answer loud and clear: Don't you remember Luther's desperate struggle in the monastery? He flung himself into religious works, fasting, confessing, and punishing his body and

FINAL EVENTS ON PLANET EARTH

mind by installment in an unplanned suicide. Frightened of Christ, he was the most miserable man on earth. Luther says, "I was so imprisoned in this practice that the Lord had to tear me from this self-torture by violence." [1] Trapped within himself, he saw no way out until Dr. Staupitz led him to see that Jesus Christ had already accepted him.

Don't listen to self. Force it to see its helplessness. Fling in its face the words, "Without me [Christ] ye can do nothing" (John 15:5, KJV). Really it is just as impossible for you to earn Christ's love as for a waterfall to flow upward, to have given yourself birth, or for a disconnected branch to bear fruit. For apart from Christ we cannot obey—we are weak. As Augustine declared, "When Thou art our strength, we have strength indeed, but when we rely upon ourselves, our strength is nothing but weakness." [2]

Away, then, with all do-it-yourself religion. Instead, rejoice in the fact that Christ died for you before you were born and that His death is the greatest proof that He accepts you just as you are.

"Ah," speaks up another, "now you are talking down my alley. Jesus Christ did everything for us, and to that we cannot add one iota. Then all we have to do is believe, isn't it? We do not have to do anything else, do we?"

"A thousand times no!" responds the answer of love straining at the leash. Remember the character Hopeful in John Bunyan's dream? He had almost given up because of his vileness till he met Jesus Christ and looked away from self to Him. Then he discovered the wonderful fact that Christ

ARE YOU WEAK?

accepted him. But did he take it easy, just believing while doing nothing? Not a bit. In utter gratitude to Christ he exclaimed, "Had I now a thousand gallons of blood in my body, I could spill it all for the sake of the Lord Jesus."[3]

That's what acceptance does—it bursts forth in grateful obedience. It cannot help it, for love has to express itself. " 'If you love me,' " Jesus said—and He might have added, "Only if you really do, for without love, obedience is a farce" (see 1 Corinthians 13:3)—" 'If you love me, you will keep my commandments' " (John 14:15, RSV). Obedience constitutes more than belief, for Jesus also declared, "He who believes in me will also do the works that I do" (John 14:12, RSV).

Remember, too, that a Christian is a branch grafted to the Vine; so it naturally becomes Vinelike. As Andrew Murray expressed it, "No one who learns to rest upon the living Christ can become slothful, for the closer your contact with Christ the more of the Spirit of His zeal and love will be borne in upon you."[4]

"Ah, but wait longer," calls a third. "You are now getting closer to my concerns. Shouldn't our whole life concentrate upon what we should do, what laws of God we should obey? Shouldn't studying the law in order to do better become our supreme task?"

Let me answer from my own experience. As a teenage lad near London, England, I stuck a list on my bedroom wall against which I made daily checks. But the harder I tried to gain victory over its items, the worse my situation became. Gulley was in a rut—a miserable failure. But why?

FINAL EVENTS ON PLANET EARTH

An unchanging law states that by beholding we become transformed (see 2 Corinthians 3:18). Looking to that chart, I only saw myself. To become like Jesus Christ I must look to Him, read about Him, meditate on His life, and commune with Him. It is a case of my setting "the Lord always before me: because he is at my right hand, I shall not be moved" (Psalm 16:8, KJV).

You see, it's not *what* you know but *whom* you know that counts. The Pharisees knew the law backward and forward, but they crucified Christ, the Lawgiver, and then ran home to keep the Sabbath. In our day many will exclaim to the returned Christ, " 'Lord, Lord, did we not prophesy in your name, and cast out demons in your name, and do many mighty works in your name?' And then will I [Christ] declare to them, 'I never knew you; depart from me, you evildoers' " (Matthew 7:22, 23, RSV). Think of it—they were so busy doing the work of the Lord that they didn't take time to know the Lord of the work. To have a relationship with Him is essential, for "this is eternal life, that they *know* thee the only true God, and Jesus Christ whom thou hast sent" (John 17:3, RSV).

The battle for victory is not over sins (or even to discover those things we do wrong without realizing it); rather, it is to become, and remain, connected with Jesus Christ, the Saviour from sin. Then God will supply the victory. "Thanks be to God, who in Christ always leads us in triumph" (2 Corinthians 2:14, RSV).

Consider the last talk Jesus Christ had with His disciples before His crucifixion. In seven

ARE YOU WEAK?

verses Jesus Christ spoke of obedience or keeping the commandments, and in three He referred to His own doing of His Father's will. He mentioned belief or believing seven times, but never once as sufficient in itself. But more important still, twenty-six times Jesus Christ spoke of Christians as *in* Him, He *in* them, including also His being *in* His Father, and His Father *in* Him. Such *union* holds the key to all else, for there we find victory (John 17:11, 15). It's not just we ourselves *keeping* the law—the Lawgiver is keeping us.

Note the heart of His final discourse when Jesus summed it all up in calling Christians to be branches growing from Him, the Vine (John 15). Does the branch sustain the vine, or the vine the branch? The Vine keeps the branches alive. He alone is able to keep us from falling (Jude 24). "No one who abides in him sins" (1 John 3:6, RSV).

Jesus, our human brother, set us the example in His life of obedience. A vine cannot stand upright by itself. It requires external support. So Jesus the Vine utterly depended on His Father. He said, "I can of mine own self do nothing" (John 5:30, KJV). "The words that I speak unto you I speak not of myself: but the Father that dwelleth in me, he doeth the works" (John 14:10, KJV).

The early church followed Christ's example. Pentecost united them to God. Weak disciples changed to powerful witnesses. Obedience became important to them. They knew not only that they obtained their salvation through the obedience of Christ (Philippians 2:8) but also that "he became the source of eternal salvation to all who obey him" (Hebrews 5:9, RSV).

FINAL EVENTS ON PLANET EARTH

Over and over again we find the early Christians filled with the Holy Spirit: Stephen (Acts 7:55), Barnabas (Acts 11:24), Paul (Acts 13:9), the disciples at Iconium (Acts 13:52) and at Ephesus (Acts 19:6). No wonder they stormed the world, shook it to its foundations, turned it upside down. Aflame for God, moved mightily by His instructing power, they passionately declared, "We ought to obey God rather than men" (Acts 5:29, KJV).

The throbbing heart of the New Testament is union with Jesus Christ. It is the source from which flows all obedience, the center of the gospel. Paul proclaimed, "I live; yet not I, but Christ liveth in me" (Galatians 2:20, KJV). The same experience can be ours, for "it is God which worketh in you both to will and to do of his good pleasure" (Philippians 2:13, KJV).

Christianity is a relationship rather than mere rules, a fellowship and not just form, for at its heart stands a Person instead of a practice. Here is the gospel's Good News for the church of the last days. A watching, working, witnessing church is one that has first become united with Jesus Christ. His friendship compels them into a vigorous, vibrant life-style that issues naturally from a connection with the Life-giver. God's control in their life provides the source for all Christian living.

Seven-year-old Harry Stage made sensational news in the *Washington Star* on February 20, 1961. Why? Twenty-five miles away from his Phoenix, Arizona, home, while his father talked to a Mr. Faubion, the boy climbed onto a platform,

ARE YOU WEAK?

saw an old piece of plywood at one side, and jumped for it. The plywood covered an irrigation well 16 inches wide and 250 feet deep.

The plywood broke. Harry plunged down, part of the plywood slowing him a little. Hitting the water, he pushed against the wall of the well with his hands to keep from submerging and yelled, "Daddy, Daddy, get me out! Daddy, Daddy . . ."

"Don't worry, Son, and don't be scared." His father thought quickly. "We'll get you out. Just push against the sides so you don't sink."

"Okay. Quick! Hurry!"

Mr. Faubion drove furiously the seven miles to a neighbor's ranch to get ropes to tie together to rescue Harry. Meanwhile the frightened seven-year-old waited. With many bad bruises, both legs broken, tiring arms, he was absolutely helpless. Would his father ever come? How much longer could he hold on? Would he drown? When finally the men lowered the rope, he gladly followed every instruction and obeyed implicitly. Placing the rope around his body, he held on for dear life as his father and Mr. Faubion pulled him to safety.

That rope saved Harry. It brought him back to his father because he remained connected to it. We all have fallen headlong into the pit of sin. Bruised, broken, helpless, we cannot save ourselves. Although only those who obey the Father will get to the Father (Matthew 7:21), only Christ let down to us is the way out to the Father, for He said, "I am the way: . . . no man cometh unto the Father, but by me" (John 14:6, KJV). We must connect ourselves to Him. He alone resurrects us to triumphant living. His control in our lives

FINAL EVENTS ON PLANET EARTH

causes us to obey and enjoy it. "Thank God there *is* a way out through Jesus Christ our Lord" (Romans 7:25, Phillips).

---

[1] E. G. Schwiebert, *Luther and His Times* (St. Louis: Concordia, 1950), p. 150.

[2] *The Confessions of St. Augustine,* Book 4 (London: Fontana Books, Collins, 1963), p. 112.

[3] John Bunyan, *Pilgrim's Progress* (Fort Washington, Pennsylvania: Christian Literature Crusade, 1947), p. 146.

[4] Andrew Murray, *Absolute Surrender* (London: Lakeland, 1974), p. 133.

ARE YOU WEAK?

Chapter 5

What's Happening to the Nations?

A few years ago a special document prepared by Nobel prizewinning scientists went to all world leaders. It warned, "Here, then, is the problem which we present to you, stark and dreadful and inescapable: shall we put an end to the human race or shall mankind renounce war? We appeal, as human beings to human beings; remember your humanity, and forget the rest. If you can do so, the way lies open to a new paradise; if you cannot, there lies before you the risk of universal death."[1]

Modern man seems bent on war in spite of the overshadowing atomic mushroom with its threat of utter destruction. A group of Harvard University scholars heading a research of war trends came up with an astonishing discovery. During the past twenty-five hundred years they discovered over nine hundred wars and almost two thousand international disturbances. But the first quarter of the twentieth century was "the bloodiest period in all history; . . . the war index for the twentieth century was eight times greater than all preceding centuries."[2]

Like a cancer, global distress eats out the world's vitals. Few know what lies behind the feverish frenzy to shove mankind into World War III. To understand present world unrest we must penetrate to history's climax, analyze it, and find out what the real facts are. Through the coming future we can better understand the confusing present.

Many Christians believe in the battle of Armageddon but hold numerous interpretations. Most look for a Middle East conflict in Palestine's Megiddo. Multitudes nervously scan the Israeli-Arab situation as the explosive center to ignite world destruction. Russia and America uneasily watch their vested interests there. The oil stakes are high. But the Bible has a totally different viewpoint. Scripture speaks of Armageddon as the ultimate climax—not between East and West but between the world and God's people. It is a religious struggle, not political. Historian Dr. Arnold J. Toynbee exposed the root crisis of today when he affirmed, "The fundamental conflict is not political but religious; and the dividing line between the two religious camps is not the present world-encompassing political boundary between Russian and an American sphere of political influence. The line cuts across the inward spiritual world within every living soul today—whatever label of political citizenship may have been stamped on its body by the accident of birth."[3] Seventh-day Adventists believe the world is fast polarizing into two bodies—those against God and those for Him.

The well-used Armageddon passage, Revelation 16:12-16, did not arise in a vacuum. Its roots go back through at least seventeen Biblical books

FINAL EVENTS ON PLANET EARTH

clear to Genesis. Revelation comprises a veritable mosaic of Old Testament allusions and references —some six hundred of them. Without a thorough knowledge of the Old Testament you will lose much of the meaning of the book, including that of Armageddon.

The Reformers' principle of *sola scriptura* (interpreting the Bible by Scripture only) is the key to unlock Revelation. We should go to the Bible and not to passing political history for the interpretation of Armageddon. To look beyond Scripture is to step outside of the canon and to engage in producing apocrypha.

In coming to the Bible, one asks it to reveal its own inner rationality rather than superimposing on it any alien presupposition of the researcher. The Bible is a book that operates according to definite laws of interpretation, just as nature does. To discover and apply them will unlock the mystery of Armageddon and help us understand what is happening to the nations today.

One principle that emerges from Bible study is that a local happening often typifies something worldwide in scope. For example, Jerusalem's destruction is a type of the coming world destruction (Matthew 24). The same is true of Armageddon. The local root reference to Megiddo appears in Judges 4 and 5. Israel had suffered twenty years of oppression (4:3) under many nations confederated together (Psalm 83:1-10). God promised deliverance (Judges 4:6-9), and every enemy soldier perished (4:16). The Lord avenged Israel (5:2) at the battle of Megiddo (5:19), and the land

WHAT'S HAPPENING TO THE NATIONS?

had rest for forty years (5:31).

Here we find that Israel—as God's people and not as a political entity—is the focus of attack and of deliverance. Many years later history repeated itself. God's people faced another local Armageddon. A great multitude of nations surrounded Israel (2 Chronicles 20:1, 2). Judah, under Jehoshaphat, sought God in utter helplessness (verses 3, 12). And the Lord said, " 'Fear not, and be not dismayed at this great multitude; for the battle is not yours but God's' " (20:15, RSV). " 'Fear not, and be not dismayed; tomorrow go out against them, and the Lord will be with you' " (verse 17). The next day strong soldiers sang the doxology—didn't fight—and God won the battle. Not one of the enemy escaped (verses 21-24).

Time passed, and so did Israel—into captivity to Babylon. But God was ready for the emergency. More than a century before, He prophesied that Cyrus would be His instrument to deliver Israel from Babylon (Isaiah 45-47). Babylon would be overthrown in "one day" (47:9), the same language used of spiritual Babylon in Armageddon's battle (Revelation 18:8). Just as literal Israel triumphed over literal Babylon, so will spiritual Israel (the church) have victory over spiritual Babylon (the enemy of the church). And the arrival of Cyrus to save Israel from Babylon symbolized Christ's advent to save spiritual Israel.

Each of the above references is a separate unfolding of the struggle between good and evil. Satan has attempted to destroy God's people through the ages, and in the coming Armageddon he will launch his final, universal assault. Spiri-

FINAL EVENTS ON PLANET EARTH

tual Israel is worldwide today; so Armageddon will be global. Armageddon has to do with salvation history and not just with international strife.

In the middle of the Armageddon passage (Revelation 16) Christ says, " 'Lo, I am coming like a thief! Blessed is he who is awake, keeping his garments that he may not go naked and be seen exposed!' " (verse 15). It is the same message given to the Laodicean church (Revelation 3:18). Here we have an amplification of God's appeal to His last church to wear Christ's robes of righteousness. Only those Christ has delivered from sin will He rescue from Armageddon (Daniel 12:1). Christ will stand up only for those who have stood up for Him. Physical deliverance follows spiritual. The call to come to Christ and let His life cover you rings loud and clear from the strife that tears at the nations. Soon it will be too late.

Satan's studied strategy is to take over the world and destroy God's people. The Bible says, "And I saw, issuing from the mouth of the dragon and from the mouth of the beast and from the mouth of the false prophet, three foul spirits like frogs; for they are demonic spirits, performing signs, who go abroad to the kings of the whole world, to assemble them for battle on the great day of God the Almighty" (Revelation 16:13, 14, RSV).

Through his three instrumentalities Satan assembles his hordes. At the same time the three angels' messages (Revelation 14) represent three means through which God appeals to His followers still in spiritual Babylon to come over to spiritual Israel. A double gathering is thus in progress. Both move inexorably toward the final battle.

WHAT'S HAPPENING TO THE NATIONS?

The devil does everything possible to stop persons crossing over from his ranks to God's. But even if they do, he aims to crush them; for "the dragon was angry with the woman [church], and went off to make war on the rest of her offspring" (Revelation 12:17, RSV). The passage is the first of many Armageddon texts in Revelation. They repeat and enlarge on the original one, speaking of a war against God and His people, not just an international battle. The whole world will marvel at the beast (Revelation 13:3) and pass a death decree to annihilate God's people (Revelation 13:15, 17). But rescue will come. "He that sat on the cloud thrust in his sickle on the earth; and the earth was reaped" (Revelation 14:16, KJV).

The root of the latter verse appears in Joel 3. There God warns, "I will also gather all nations, and will bring them down into the valley of Jehoshaphat: . . . for there will I sit to judge all the heathen round about. Put ye in the sickle, for the harvest is ripe: come, get you down; for the press is full, the fats overflow, for their wickedness is great" (verses 2, 12, 13, KJV).

The Old Testament allusion, found again in the third angel's message (Revelation 14:6, 7), receives additional amplification in Revelation 19:11-21. Here John compares Christ to One leading an army of horsemen. "Then I saw heaven opened, and behold, a white horse! He who sat upon it is called Faithful and True, and in righteousness he judges and makes war. . . . And the armies of heaven, arrayed in fine linen, white and pure, followed him on white horses. From his mouth issues a sharp sword with which to smite

FINAL EVENTS ON PLANET EARTH

the nations, and he will rule them with a rod of iron. . . . On his robe and on his thigh he has a name inscribed, King of kings and Lord of lords. . . . And I saw the beast and the kings of the earth with their armies gathered to make war against him who sits upon the horse and against his army. And the beast was captured, and with it the false prophet who in its presence had worked the signs by which he deceived those who had received the mark of the beast. . . . These two were thrown alive into the lake of fire that burns with sulphur" (Revelation 19:11-20, RSV).

The world hurtles toward its shocking climax. But the four angels hold back total chaos (Revelation 7:1, 4). When they loosen the symbolic winds of strife, Satan will have "entire control of the finally impenitent."[4] Then God's followers will find themselves plunged into what the Bible calls Jacob's trouble, a crisis worse than any they have ever experienced before (Daniel 12:1). As Jacob feared death at the hand of Esau (Genesis 32:6-12), so they will come under a death decree to eradicate them in one swoop (Revelation 13:15). But God will protect them just as He did Jacob, and just as He did His people in the local Armageddons of the past (Daniel 12:1).

"After the saints had been delivered by the voice of God, the wicked multitude turned their rage upon one another. The earth seemed to be deluged with blood, and dead bodies were from one end to the other."[5] "The people see that they have been deluded. They accuse one another of having led them to destruction; but all unite in heaping their bitterest condemnation upon the ministers.

WHAT'S HAPPENING TO THE NATIONS?

... The swords which were to slay God's people are now employed to destroy their enemies. Everywhere there is strife and bloodshed." [6]

Then the angel of death will do his work. He "goes forth, represented in Ezekiel's vision by the men with the slaughtering weapons, to whom the command is given: 'Slay utterly old and young, both maids, and little children, and women.' " [7] Finally, "at the coming of Christ the wicked are blotted from the face of the whole earth—consumed with the spirit of His mouth and destroyed by the brightness of His glory." [8]

The bloodiest war of the century, and of all time, approaches. But God will sustain His own, just as He has in the past. He is in control of the coming climax and gathers His people from enemy territory. Just as the Jews escaped through the Exodus to go to their own land, and just as Israel returned to Palestine out of Babylonian captivity, so God's children will leave spiritual Babylon. That joyous future—and not atomic annihilation—is the sure hope of the faithful.

[1] Bertrand Russell, *Has Man a Future?* (New York: Simon and Schuster, 1962), quoted in Lindsey, *The Late Great Planet Earth,* p. 147.

[2] Louis F. Were, *Europe and Armageddon* (125 Waverly Road, East Malvern, Australia: A. T. Blackburn, printer, preface dated 1949), pp. 37f.

[3] Cited by Francis D. Nichol in *Our Firm Foundation* (Washington, D.C.: Review and Herald Publishing Association, 1953), Vol. 1, p. 612.

[4] Ellen G. White, *The Great Controversy* (Mountain View, California: Pacific Press Publishing Association, 1950), p. 614.

[5] Ellen G. White, *Early Writings* (Washington, D.C.: Review and Herald Publishing Association, 1945), p. 290.

[6] *The Great Controversy,* pp. 655, 656.

[7] *Ibid.,* p. 656.

[8] *Ibid.,* p. 657.

Chapter 6

Who Has Your Mind?

The death-decree (Revelation 13:15) generation is here![1]

"No generation growing up in any epoch of history or in any place has had to face such a deluge of violence as modern American youth, now old enough to make history itself."[2]

A report to the Federal Communication Commission states that "between the ages of five and fourteen the average American child witnesses the violent destruction of thirteen thousand human beings on television."[3]

The U.S. Senate subcommittee investigated the possible relationship between juvenile delinquency and crime on TV. The chairman, Senator Thomas Dodd of Connecticut, concluded, "Glued to the TV set from the time they can walk, our children are getting an intensive training in all phases of crime from the ever-increasing array of Westerns and crime-detective programs available to them. The past decade has seen TV come of age. However, the same decade has witnessed the violence content in programs skyrocket and delinquency in real life grow almost 200 percent."[4]

Stanford University research of four TV channels in one American city revealed the shocking fact that even "the children's hour is heavy in physical violence, light in intellectual interchange, and deeply concerned with crime."[5]

Little wonder that the TV box houses the world's largest "school for violence." One concerned writer asked, "What will happen to a generation raised upon such an idea?" He went on to answer his own question. "We do not know, because today's children are the first guinea pigs."[6]

Bible students know that such a generation could vote for the death decree on God's people. It happened back in the Roman amphitheater, where packed crowds roared approval when mangled, broken bodies drew their last breath under the fangs and claws of wild beasts. A generation raised on violence is with us. Murder is their daily diet—why not some more in the final death decree?

The average person in America absorbs twenty hours of such TV each week.[7] Minds are crumbling. Without reading, thinking, and creativity, mental shrinkage is as real as is muscular. Spend a month in bed, and how strong are your legs? Millions of minds "are in bed"—nearly dormant, merely passive, as they sit glued to the box. "Sluggish conformity" has resulted.[8] Put "love of violence" and "sluggish conformity" together, and you are all set for the universal death decree—when all will conform to attempt to kill the few innocent. After all, it will be entertainment.[9]

The death decree will be international. Peoples of every nation will vote to exterminate God's

FINAL EVENTS ON PLANET EARTH

followers. The final violent generation will be worldwide. Through Hollywood and television American influence has reached the remotest corners. Westerns are popular in the Orient. And crime movies attract audiences everywhere. As movie critic Hollis Alpert puts it, "The conviction that crime pays off at the box office is firmly entrenched in Hollywood."[10]

American commercial influence also affects most of the world. Dr. Herbert Schiller, University of California professor, remarked, "No part of the globe (except, and perhaps only temporarily, the socialist-organized sector) avoids the penetration of the internationally active American advertising agency."[11] "In fact," he continued, "the expansion of American advertising agencies is accelerating, increasingly bringing foreign competitors under the American umbrella."[12]

"Communication control"[13] is the "in thing," welding the world's masses more and more into one. Ben H. Bagdikian puts it, "The men who control these instruments of communication have enormous power. Where once priests and kings decided what the populace would hear, the proprietors of the mass media now decide."[14]

Robert Sarnoff, chairman of the Board of RCA, called for a "global common market of communications."[15] Global control through mass media is thus a possibility in our time. If men fear atomic power, they should equally cower under the thrust of mass media. In different ways both can prove as equally devastating. In his book *Crisis in Television* Solomon Simonson takes the position that "there is no escape from either the pursuing bomb

WHO HAS YOUR MIND?

or the omnipresent television." [16]

Robert Stein, in *Media Power,* asserts that "it is as futile to lament the effects of Media Power as it is to bewail the destructive potential of nuclear fission. Neither will be 'disinvented.' Both require sophistication and social responsibility." [17]

In *Violence and the Mass Media,* edited by Otto N. Larsen, a report of TV viewing habits from the Bureau of Applied Social Research of Columbia University revealed that only 5 percent of parents regulate the programs their children watch. Adults regard the amount of time spent rather than what the children view as the more important consideration. "Apparently, most of us are using television as a baby-sitter, and not bothering to ask for references. We do not reflect that this particular sitter may be a wicked influence." [18]

Mind damage through TV is as destructive as the physical desolation of Hiroshima and Nagasaki. "It is a law both of the intellectual and the spiritual nature that by beholding we become changed. The mind gradually adapts itself to the subjects upon which it is allowed to dwell." [19] Little by little, through TV watching, Satan transforms the multitudes in his bid to take over humanity. But he is working on more than one front.

Bob Larson, onetime rock musician, feels convinced that Satan seeks to get the youth through music. "Hard rock is the agency which Satan is using to possess this generation *en masse.* I have seen with my own eyes teenagers who have become demon-possessed while dancing to rock music. It was particularly noticeable with girls. One might expect a young lady to maintain some decency while dancing, but I have seen teenage girls go through contortions that could only be the manifestation of demon activity.... On Friday and Saturday nights across America the devil is gaining demonic control over thousands of teenage lives."[20]

The name of the game is *control*. Whether through TV, other mass media, or through hard rock music, Satan hopes to bring the world into *True* conformity to his plans. It is a sophisticated form of demon possession—but just as ugly and tragic.

The *Encyclopaedia Britannica* mentions that "the therapeutic possession dances of Africa have spread to the new world, as in the *candomblé* of Brazil, the *winti* of Surinam (Dutch Guinea) and the *vodun* of Trinidad and Haiti. In these dances an African deity enters a devotee and produces frenzied dancing in the character of the god."[21] No wonder *Time* magazine dubbed the Woodstock rock festival as a "rhythmic orgasm."[22] Hypnotized by the beat, the participants little realize what they are doing.

Multitudes have until recently laughed Satan out of existence. Even some Christian theologians have dismissed the reality of the devil, but he is, as Hal Lindsey's book title puts it, "alive and well on Planet Earth."

Well in body maybe—but sick in mind. He seeks to degrade and destroy through abject control. While former archbishop of Canterbury, Michael Ramsey, could say "fiddlesticks" to most supposed demonic possessions[23] and prominent psychiatrist William Bellamy dismissed such possessions as a " 'delusion' and an example of

WHO HAS YOUR MIND?

'schizophrenia,' "[24] the devil plunges on. More recently, however, books and movies such as *The Exorcist* have flooded the market, and in some surveys the number of people expressing a belief in the devil has passed that of those believing in God.

Satan watches constantly to destroy.[25] He is out "to gain control of the whole mind."[26] The devil knows that "it is the mind that worships God, and allies us to heavenly beings."[27] And he recognizes that only the mind "elevates man above the beasts."[28] If he can knock it out, he has broken man's only contact with God and reduced him to the animal level. He doesn't care by what means he accomplishes his end. Mind-blasting drugs, TV, mass media, rock music, or any other workable tool suits him well.

One might say, "But none of the above affect me. Am I safe, then?" But we must remember that "the mind is controlled either by Satan or by Jesus."[29]

Here are two ways to know our status: (1) "Unless you cultivate a cheerful, happy, grateful frame of mind, Satan will eventually lead you captive at his will."[30] (2) "Satan well knows that all whom he can lead to neglect prayer and the searching of the Scriptures, will be overcome by his attacks. Therefore he invents every possible device to engross the mind."[31]

Crafty? Definitely! He will get those not occupied by the best as well as those immersed in the worst. Because I don't watch TV crime stories or listen to objectionable music doesn't mean a thing if I do not spend time in prayer, Bible study,

FINAL EVENTS ON PLANET EARTH

and in being optimistic. The ugly devalues the mind, and the beautiful ennobles it. The mind cannot stand still, just not doing anything. It must be active in good if we are to be safe. Scripture tells of the man out of whom the devil was cast, but when nothing took its place, the individual received seven other devils who jumped aboard to fill the vacuum. The one who fills your mind controls it.

---

[1] Although the decree will result from international crises and Satan's appearance as Christ promising solutions if humanity will execute the Sabbathkeepers, Satan already works hard to prepare the masses to make that decision.

[2] *Violence and the Mass Media,* ed. by Otto N. Larsen (New York: Harper and Row, 1968), p. 51.

[3] *Ibid.,* p. 41.

[4] *Ibid.,* p. 43.

[5] *Ibid.,* p. 41.

[6] *Ibid.,* p. 42.

[7] Solomon Simonson, *Crisis in Television* (New York: Living Books, 1966), p. 9.

[8] *Ibid.,* p. 15.

[9] It will be more than that—it will be for survival. With nuclear holocaust seemingly inevitable, Satan's appeal (as Christ) to kill the few Sabbathkeepers to ensure peace will seem wise counsel.

[10] *Saturday Review,* August 5, 1967, quoted in Kyle Haselden's *Morality and the Mass Media* (Nashville: Broadman, 1968), p. 158.

[11] Herbert Schiller, *The Mind Managers* (Boston: Beacon Press, 1973), p. 129.

[12] *Ibid.,* p. 130.

[13] *Ibid.,* p. 145.

[14] Ben H. Bagdikian, *The Information Machines, Their Impact on Men and the Media* (New York: Harper and Row, 1971), p. xii.

[15] Schiller, *op. cit.,* p. 144f.

[16] Simonson, *op. cit.,* p. 8.

[17] Robert Stein, *Media Power: Who Is Shaping Your Picture of the World?* (Boston: Houghton Mifflin Co., 1972), p. xvii.

[18] *Violence and the Mass Media,* p. 43.

WHO HAS YOUR MIND?

[19] *The Great Controversy,* p. 555.

[20] Bob Larson, *Rock and the Church* (Illinois: Creation House, 1971), p. 68f.

[21] *Encyclopaedia Britannica* (Chicago: William Benton, 1971), Vol. 7, p. 39.

[22] *Time,* April 13, 1970, p. 103.

[23] *The Register*, Napa, California, January 31, 1974.

[24] *Ibid.,* January 19, 1974.

[25] Ellen G. White, *Life Sketches* (Mountain View: Pacific Press Publishing Association, 1943), p. 291.

[26] *The Great Controversy,* p. 489.

[27] Ellen G. White, *Fundamentals of Christian Education* (Nashville: Southern Publishing Association, 1923), p. 426.

[28] Ellen G. White, *Testimonies for the Church* (Mountain View, California: Pacific Press Publishing Association, 1948), Vol. 8, p. 127.

[29] *Ibid.,* Vol. 4, p. 495.

[30] *Ibid.,* Vol. 1, p. 704.

[31] *The Great Controversy,* p. 519.

FINAL EVENTS ON PLANET EARTH

Chapter 7

Is Your Family in Orbit?

"I think we are in the beginning of another evolution in the history of man. Probably never before have so many people been so discouraged and dissatisfied with the state of the human condition as now. Everywhere, there are huge pockets of people demanding change. The main cry seems to be for greater feelings of individual self-esteem."[1] The preceding statement, made by Virginia Satir, comes from the chapter "The Family of the Future" in her book *Peoplemaking*. But what kind of people will we see in the future?

Virginia Satir envisages that the future family may take on various forms. Society will not consider divorce, illegitimate birth, and homosexuality as morally bad but merely "evidence of the great variations in human beings." Persons will make their own marriage contracts of from one to five years to renew or dissolve thereafter as they will. Humanity will accept polygamy and communal marriage. Virginia Satir sees such a future as the development of "a more responsible human being."[2]

It is high time we come to grips with the utterly horrifying possibilities ahead for the world if we do not fight for the family. "Peoplemaking" is best done, not according to humanly devised patterns, but by the one given by God—the nuclear family comprised of two parents and their children. He who made us knows best about our needs. All other plans result from eroding ethical behavior.

Many couples hardly ever get into the orbit of family success because they never really had a proper launching. What do we mean? Astronauts are not just ordinary pilots but individuals with additional training and preparation for their mission. NASA would never choose me to command a space module—they have more sense than to waste so much on someone who knows nothing about the task. But families are not just things— they are the fabric of society. And yet how many people attempt to form one without adequate preparation. Much of the reason for divorce lies right here.

Study indicates, for example, that earlier marriages will less likely succeed.[3] On the other hand, a 1968 study revealed that doctors in California who married after completing their medical training had comparatively low divorce rates.[4] Thorough preparation before launching will help achieve successful orbiting—and that includes mental and spiritual maturity besides physical readiness. Wide reading on the subject of family responsibilities, some money to start on, a steady job—all undergirded by a deep commitment to God—help give good preparation. Just as qualified pilots with the right training make astronauts, so people plus preparation lead to candidates ready for launching into marriage.

FINAL EVENTS ON PLANET EARTH

Tandem bikes are made for two. So are wedding vows, till death absolves them. They form a commitment, not just a contract. Two people become as one. Unless a genuine, growing oneness merges the original two, we can expect little likelihood of unity in the wider extension between parents and children.

Never take your partner for granted. Love is won not only in courtship but throughout life. Why does the spring joy so soon turn to winter chill? Not spending sufficient time together causes a couple to drift apart. Share yourselves with each other every day, get to know each other better, just plain listen to each other. Don't forget the little attentions, the thoughtful words, the acts of kindness, which say so eloquently to the other, "I love you."

High above the launching pad, at least a nine-month journey into the future, the first child may join the family circle. Now the two that became one have become one again in a third. Research studies have shown that children can bring happiness to marriage.[5] But they need emotional satisfaction that can come only from parents. Parents provide many needs for their children, but <u>more than things, children require their</u> ✓ <u>parents'</u> *presence* <u>more than their</u> *presents*.

A mother visited her son in the Memorial Guidance Clinic in Richmond, Virginia. She brought him an expensive camera, since it was his eighth birthday. Seeing her, the lad ran to snuggle up to her as eight-year-olds will. "Keep away," the mother cried. "You'll rumple my dress." She left with her evening dress unrumpled. A broken-

IS YOUR FAMILY IN ORBIT?

hearted boy soon smashed his new camera to bits.[6] Parents, you brought your children into the world. They came helpless, and they must have your companionship. Presents can never substitute for parents.

Children must stand high on the parents' priority list. Mrs. J. W. Mecom, wife of a wealthy oil magnate in Texas, didn't forget the rights and needs of hers. When approached by a delegation to bring her yard up to par with the garden club standard, she replied, "I will—after the children grow up. Right now they want it for a baseball diamond."[7]

When parents love and accept each other, they create a climate for loving and accepting their children. Such is not an ordinary family but one where fellowship constantly grows.

Anne Battle-Sister states that there is "no female culture," and that women may avoid the mistakes of "cultural nationalism."[8] How about "family nationalism"? The family is more important than culture—for culture results from the family. Many mothers, when asked their occupation, reply, "Oh! I'm just a housewife." But you should dump the word *just*. Fling your shoulders back, lift up your head, look the world in the eye—you're a mother! It is a high calling, a tremendous challenge. For did not Jesus Christ have a mother, Mary? and Moses, Jochebed? Think of the contribution both made to their sons.

My mother was an editorial secretary, and she thoroughly enjoyed writing articles. It was her pleasure to work for Arthur S. Maxwell when he served as editor of Stanborough Press near

FINAL EVENTS ON PLANET EARTH

London, England. But a day arrived when she heard the call of motherhood and laid down the pen to take up washing, cleaning, cooking, and the other endless jobs around the home. I don't ever remember seeing an article from Mother's pen during my growing-up years, but I did see *her*. My brother and I never came home to an empty house, for the mother who saw us off in the morning was there when we arrived in the afternoon. But countless thousands of children return to empty houses, and they become empty inside themselves. Television, bad company, and idleness destroy them. Mothers, why opt for your so-called liberation at the expense of your children's enslavement?

Child raising is just as much a parental partnership as getting them in the first place. Children, a product of both father and mother, need both parents. Though the mother should spend more time with the children, her companionship can never substitute for the father's. As one boy blurted, "Daddy, Mother is wonderful and she means a lot to me, but sometimes she forgets how she felt when she was a boy."

Have you ever heard the phrase: "The family that prays together stays together"? It's up to you, Dad. You are the spiritual guide of the home, the leader in family worship. If God is truly the center of a home, then in approaching Him, the members will come closer to one another. You've seen how spokes in a wheel meet at the hub. That's the way it is in a Christian home.

Up there in orbit, traveling together requires mutual thinking and planning. Deciding on

IS YOUR FAMILY IN ORBIT?

projects and games interesting to all helps to keep any from drifting off by themselves. A family council can convene once a week, administered by a different family member each time. It could discuss such items as (1) deciding what to do for family day (one designated afternoon or evening a week); (2) sharing of coming plans; (3) airing of questions or problems for answers and solutions. Such a meeting can help make children feel that they are participating members of the family rather than second-class citizens carrying out orders. They will have a sense of belonging.

The family council lets parents and children meet as equals—sharing their hopes, frustrations, and joys. It provides a window for parents to look into, and thus understand, their children. But it also allows children to see their parents as genuine friends.

Basic to such a council is the desire to make the other members happy. <u>Happiness doesn't come to those who seek it—only to those who give it, for happiness is never a goal in itself. It results as a by-product of making others happy.</u> As it is true within the family circle, so is it in the larger social circle too. The family council can plan projects for poorer families or for the crippled or the aged in the neighborhood.

Once launched, rockets require continued thrust or they will plunge back to earth and destruction. The religious beginning in prayer and commitment in the church wedding service needs to remain the basic daily flight fuel, providing power to lift the family through any turbulence. Man is spiritual as well as mental and physical.

FINAL EVENTS ON PLANET EARTH

Although the United States Constitution rightly keeps church and state separate, the spiritual needs of each family member must never remain isolated from mental and physical necessities. Such division constitutes one of the primary reasons for family failure.

The president of the Family Association of America, Walter Barlowe, recently declared, "The ultimate survival of our society depends on the quality of our families."[9] To that end Dr. Vincent M. Rue of the University of North Carolina proposed the creation of a Cabinet-status United States Department of Marriage and the Family. The same needs exist in varying degrees in all countries of the world.[10]

Many are trying to keep their families in orbit, but the downward pull is strong. Countless families crash. Why not, before it's too late, propose a family council in your home in which all members can enter into the exciting exploration of working, playing, and praying together? And God as the center of the family provides safety, for His control preserves, builds up, and develops the family unit to its ultimate potential. Such families the church urgently needs during the last days.

---

[1] Virginia Satir, *Peoplemaking* (Palo Alto, California: Science and Behavior Books, Inc., 1972), p. 303.

[2] *Ibid.,* pp. 298-304.

[3] As, for example, *Journal of Marriage and the Family,* February, 1974, pp. 72-75.

[4] *Ibid.,* November, 1972, pp. 587-598.

[5] *Ibid.,* February, 1970, p. 43f.

[6] W. T. Thompson, *Adventures in Parenthood,* p. 41.

[7] *Ibid.,* p. 35.

IS YOUR FAMILY IN ORBIT?

[8]*Journal of Marriage and the Family,* August, 1971, pp. 411-420.

[9]Farson, Richard E., *et al., The Future of the Family* (New York: Family Service Assoc. of America, 44 East 23rd Street, 1969), p. 78.

[10]*Journal of Marriage and the Family,* November, 1973, pp. 689-699.

FINAL EVENTS ON PLANET EARTH

Chapter 8

Is Revelation
on the Rocks?

The sun shone brilliantly in the beautiful old city of Basel, Switzerland. The tramcars edged their way down the center of the streets, taking people to work. A little off the main thoroughfare, in a moderately sized house, I climbed the stairs to Karl Barth's study. It was October, 1969, and I sat alone, looking at all the theological books stacked high on every side. I scanned shelves of books authored by Karl Barth, considered by many scholars as the greatest theologian of the twentieth century and one of the most profound of all time. Other shelves held scores of books written about him.

On his study table a Greek New Testament lay open. I leafed through it and found many places underlined. In that room Karl Barth had spent countless thousands of hours poring over the Bible and other books, working out his theological system which fills thirteen volumes. Dr. Barth had come a long way since university graduation in 1908.

Back in 1908 he became an associate editor of the *Christliche Welt.* For two years he followed the thought forms of Schleiermacher and Ritschl, the leading liberal theologians of the nineteenth century. But when in 1911 Barth went to the pastoral ministry at Safenwill and ascended the pulpit on Sunday morning, he realized that he had nothing to give to the people. It dawned on him that his whole university training had left him out of touch with the realities of preaching.

The predicament forced him to begin deep study of the Bible. He went to Paul's writings and in Romans, Corinthians, and Ephesians discovered what he called "the new world in the Bible." He explained it as "the Word in the word." By that he meant that Jesus Christ is revelation rather than the words of the Bible. To him Biblical words are merely signposts that point to Jesus Christ as the Word. The Bible is an encounter with Christ, not a volume of propositional facts or data.

Therefore, the Bible merely introduces the reader to revelation, pointing away from itself to the dynamic revealing activity of Jesus Christ. Revelation is present in the reaction of Jesus Christ with the reader rather than in the words of Scripture itself. This concept became the basic presupposition of neoorthodoxy or neo-Protestantism, which in its earlier days found such men as Karl Barth, Emil Brunner, Rudolf Bultmann, and Edward Thurneysen together in their attack against the liberal position of the nineteenth century which looked within man himself for revelation.

They particularly directed their attack against Friedrich Schleiermacher, the most influential theologian of the nineteenth century. Schleiermacher considered that David Hume and Immanuel Kant had effectively thrown into question the traditional objective proofs for God's existence. He felt that one could no longer prove the reality of God through nature.

Simply put, the argument went as follows: One classical proof for God's existence had been the argument from design. Just as one beholding a watch believes that it is the product of a watch-maker, so in observing the orderly universe we conclude that it is the handiwork of a wise God. Nineteenth-century scholarship rejected the conclusion on the basis that while we can still see watchmakers making watches, we cannot today see God in the process of creating.

With the objective proofs supposedly removed, how could man prove God's existence? Only the subjective area remained. Humanity must look within itself, which is precisely what Kant did. Viewing man as a moral being, he latched onto humanity's moral distinction over other creatures as evidence for a moral God. In similar fashion Schleiermacher found within himself a feeling of absolute dependence upon God and therefore concluded that God must exist.

In this setting revelation resided within the experience of the individual rather than within the Bible. For example, Schleiermacher rejected the Trinity of the Bible because he could not feel God as three beings within him. He felt only one God within. Likewise he discarded the Second Coming because all one can feel is the present and not the future. In the same way one discards the virgin birth, for who today can feel something that happened centuries ago? And so

IS REVELATION ON THE ROCKS?

the nineteenth-century leading theologian rejected Biblical revelation by placing man's experience above the written word of God in the Bible.

As I sat in Karl Barth's study I knew, in part, that it was against Schleiermacher's theology that Barth had spent his life in writing his system. Rather than looking within man, Barth looked away to the God-man, Jesus Christ. But was it an improvement? Or was Barth still in a subjective trap?

To answer our question, we need to understand the tremendous influence that Greek thought has had in the Western world, for Greek thinking has influenced the modern understanding of revelation.

Platonic dualism postulated the existence of two worlds. The world of the gods, or that of ideas, is the real one. By contrast, the sphere of matter, the world of man, is unreal. The latter merely reflects the former real world. Greek philosophy spoke in terms of the *kosmos noeton* and the *kosmos aisthēton* being separated by a *chorizsma,* or an unbridgeable gulf. In other words, the distance between the two worlds is so great that one can never cross it. Consequently, the god of the world beyond could never reveal himself to ours. Therefore, Greek philosophy had no room for revelation.

Into such concepts arose Western thought. Surprising as it may seem, in some areas, the dualistic world view has profoundly affected even Christian thought. One example of the latter is the state-of-the-dead doctrine. With the idea that the soul is eternal and therefore belongs to the world beyond at death, while the body is temporal and part of man's world, we find the outworking of Greek dualism.

But what about revelation? Has Greek thought also influenced it? Karl Barth's understanding of revelation removes it from the Bible and places it within the encountering of Jesus Christ. The resulting dichotomy between the Word of God (Jesus Christ) and the Word of God (the Bible) compares to that between the spheres of God and man. In other words, revelation does not enter the Bible just as in Greek dualism God does not come into the physical world.

Much of modern Protestant theology shares Barth's understanding of revelation.[1] Thus a large part of Protestantism no longer looks to the Bible as its authority. Authority resides in Jesus Christ rather than in the Scriptural text, within the encounter with Jesus Christ rather than within the Bible. The Bible thus gets set aside. Emil Brunner could even call it a "paper Pope." In actuality the center of religious authority shifts from Scripture to each individual.

What about the Catholic position on revelation? The second document of Vatican II, pages 111-128, seems to support revelation as residing in the Bible. But Catholic theology regards the Bible (New Testament) as the product of the church rather than the church as the result of the Bible (New Testament). True, the Christian community preceded the New Testament, the apostolic writers belonging to it. However, Catholic theology considers the church as an extension or

IS REVELATION ON THE ROCKS?

"prolongation" of the Incarnation, with Jesus Christ "handing over"[2] His kingly, priestly, and prophetic functions to the apostles, and they to their successors. Post-Apostolic tradition receives equal place with Apostolic tradition, which forms one part of revelation. Thus "the treasure of revelation" is "entrusted to the Church."[3] It follows that "the Catholic Church has been endowed with all divinely revealed truth,"[4] which is why "the task of authentically interpreting the word of God, whether written or handed on, has been entrusted exclusively to the living teaching office of the Church, whose authority is exercised in the name of Jesus Christ."[5] And so revelation, and particularly its interpretation, occurs in the church rather than in the Bible alone. The church acts in place of the Holy Spirit as interpreter of Scripture.

If in Protestantism the individual has taken the place of the Bible, in Catholicism the church has taken Scripture's role to some extent. For many in Protestantism, revelation resides in the encounter experience with Jesus Christ, whereas in Catholicism it rests, for all practical purposes, in the church. Thus Protestantism and Catholicism share a similar subjective authority over the objective revelation of God in the Bible.

Behind Protestant and Catholic formulations on revelation lies their Christology, or doctrine, which spells out the relationship of the divine with the human in Jesus Christ, the ultimate revelation of God to man. Although major differences exist between Protestant and Catholic interpretation, and also between Lutheran and Reformed

Protestant ones, many Protestant and Catholic Christologies do have a common bond—their separating the divine from the human more than a proper Incarnation requires.

Thus, Karl Barth has a "wholly other" God even in his developed Christology. Emil Brunner denies the virgin birth, making Christ too divine. The Immaculate Conception of Catholic theology, with its need for Mary and saints to intercede with Christ for men, again removes Christ from the world of men more than He should be. It would take us too far from our topic to say more about Christology, but perhaps we have brought out enough to show the distancing of Christ from our world more than He should be, which echoes Greek dualism.

By contrast, the Bible speaks of Jesus as "the Word [that] became flesh" (see John 1:1-14, RSV), entering within our world of space and time. He who was God became also man to redeem humanity and to reveal the Father (Acts 4:12; John 14:9). Scripture also says that "men moved by the Holy Spirit spoke from God" (2 Peter 1:21, RSV) to write the Bible. Nowhere does the Bible say that the Scriptures are not revelation or that they only "contain" revelation. Rather, it is understood that the Bible *is* revelation.

The Living Word, Jesus Christ, crossed the bridge between God and man, as did also the Written Word, the Bible. Both are revelations. How would we know of Jesus Christ if we had no written word? The Bible does point to Jesus Christ, but only because it is itself revelation. Moreover, the Bible points to God. It is the place

IS REVELATION ON THE ROCKS?

where He has already chosen to make His self-revelation. It provides the criteria against which we must evaluate any other encounter, either to an individual or to the church.

Scripture combines the divine and the human, expressing God's infinite thoughts in finite human words. God's thoughts come to us through men's expressions. The Word is infallible, whereas the words are fallible; the Word exhaustless, while the words are limited. The Word is divine, but the words are human.

Just as the Living Word of God came from heaven veiled in humanity to reveal His Father, so the Written Word of God came from heaven clothed in human words to present God. The thrust of both is to reveal God, but it is always accomplished through the limitations of human form. Just as the disciples found *in* Jesus Christ a revelation of God, so we as modern disciples must find God *in* the Scriptures.

Ellen White put it this way: "The Bible, with its God-given truths expressed in the language of men, presents a union of the divine and the human. Such a union existed in the nature of Christ, who was the Son of God and the Son of man. Thus it is true of the Bible, as it was of Christ, that 'the Word was made flesh, and dwelt among us' (John 1:14)."[6] Such a concept shatters all Greek dualism.

There in Barth's study the many books from Protestant and Catholic scholars had failed to break through Greek dualism to the reality of revelation *in* the Bible as it was and is *in* Jesus Christ. Just as Jesus Christ made an impact, so

FINAL EVENTS ON PLANET EARTH

has the Bible as God's written revelation. Jesus Christ and the Bible continue to carry their own authoritative credentials. What other person and what other book has had such a consistent and far-reaching influence for so many centuries?

With the charismatic movement pushing across new boundaries, spiritualism gaining new territory, and Oriental religions winning allegiance in so-called Christian communities, it is urgent that Christians wake up to their predicament. As formulated by much of modern theology, revelation is on the rocks! Little wonder that Christians have no defenses. With their rejection or downplaying of the Bible, they have turned away from the one objective basis against which they could carefully check the multitude of claims made to their subjective experience. Having jettisoned the primary source for safe decision making, they wander aimlessly—beyond the wise control of Biblical revelation.

It is time to get back to the Bible, to restore it to its proper place of authority over any individual or church. Remember the advice of Andrew Jackson: "That book, sir, is the rock on which our republic rests."

---

[1] Two exceptions are evangelicals who believe in verbal or in propositional revelation.

[2] *The Documents of Vatican II,* ed. Walter M. Abbott (London: Geoffrey Chapman, 1967), pp. 23, 40, 115, 240, 301, 348, 543f, 600ff.

[3] *Ibid.,* p. 128.

[4] *Ibid.,* p. 348.

[5] *Ibid.,* p. 117, 118.

[6] *The Great Controversy,* p. vi.

IS REVELATION ON THE ROCKS?

Chapter 9

What About the Charismatic Movement?

Is ecumenism on the rocks also? Some think it is. Thrust into orbit like an eager rocket, it has lost momentum and seems headed for premature splashdown. "Ecumenism has lost its joy" and faces an uncertain future, members of the World and National Council of Churches heard not too long ago. " 'People are asking, as never before, Is ecumenism out of date?' admitted Charles Long, U.S. executive secretary of the World Council."[1]

Marion G. Bradwell speaks of "a seeming loss of interest" in the ecumenical organizations. He believes that organic union "is slipping ground."[2] Even *The Common Catechism,* published by forty Catholic and Protestant theologians in 1975, includes a final chapter enumerating doctrines that still pose a yawning chasm between the two sides ten years after the Vatican Council.[3]

Ecumenism seemed doomed to die, but a new force thrust into the arena has turned the tide. Like a long-pent-up, now freed, gazelle, the charismatic movement leaps over denominational barriers, accomplishing more in a short time than ecumenical union committees ever achieved over the decades.

The climate was ripe for the current charismatic movement. For a hundred years, higher criticism had downgraded the Bible, dogmatic differences had splintered churches, and laymen had become disenchanted with religion, leaving the churches empty in many parts of the world. From only 14 percent who thought religion was losing its hold on American life in 1957, the number rose sharply to 54 percent in ten years, or a jump of 40 percent in just a decade. In the 1960's the "God is dead" philosophy spread among many theological circles. Religion seemed bankrupt.

Into such a cold, dead climate, the warmth of the vibrant, dynamic charismatic movement (neo-Pentecostalism) came as a welcome change. And now the experience-centered movement has burst into forty different denominations, including the major ones.

Catholic officials acknowledge the Catholic Pentecostal movement to be "the most significant current development in the Catholic Church."[4] In fact, Swiss-born theologian Dr. Walter J. Hollenweger states that the charismatic movement is growing fastest today in the Roman Catholic Church.[5] Catholic archbishop James Hayes, of Halifax, Nova Scotia, said he is "convinced that the charismatic renewal is part of that new Pentecost Pope John prayed for."[6] It has become a new kind of ecumenism, a much more effective unity movement than anything thought of before. Whereas ecumenism has been with us for much of the twentieth century with little real progress at the grass roots to show for it, the modern development has rapidly captured the imagina-

FINAL EVENTS ON PLANET EARTH

tion of thousands of laymen and brought Christians from varying churches together in an amazing way. By contrast with doctrinal formulations by the leaders, the movement has gone to the heart and drawn congregations together. By contrast to "organizational ecumenism," it has become known as "spiritual ecumenism" and has spread like a hungry fire through dry timberland.

Emmanuel Sullivan, a Franciscan friar, said that the ecumenical movement should look at the worldwide interest in the Pentecostal movement "as one of the significant signs of a way forward on the journey to rediscovering . . . full visible unity in Christ."[7] Sullivan finds in it the "essential ingredients" for full visible unity in Christ.[8] And amazingly enough, in strife-torn Ireland where Catholics and Protestants struggle in bloody conflict, they join together in charismatic prayer groups in Belfast.[9]

Time magazine stated that "while Pentecostalism is spreading like a spiritual wildfire around the world, its progress in Asia is particularly remarkable."[10] When the charismatic movement broke out in Timor Island, evangelist Mel Tari reports that people claimed to have witnessed miracles and even resurrections.[11] Japan has many Catholic charismatic prayer groups in the Kobe-Osaka area. In Korea the 10,000-capacity Full Gospel Central Church on Seoul's Yoido Island hosted the tenth Triennial Pentecostal World Conference in which fifty countries participated. Great numbers of Christians in Korea have received the so-called baptism of the Spirit, a Pentecostal experience. In the Philippines, Pentecostalism

CHARISMATIC MOVEMENT?

grows through mail-order Bible courses with fifteen hundred additional new enrollees every month.

Christianity Today has carried full-page advertisements of the book *The Beginning of the End.* Author Tim Lahaye feels conclusively that "we are living in the last generation" and that "the events of Biblical prophecy are being fulfilled completely and rapidly today." At the same time a religious leader, Norris L. Wogen, "regards the charismatic upsurge as a prelude to Christ's second coming."[12]

In the January 7, 1972, edition of *Christianity Today,* we read, "And God is setting the stage today for a great moving of his hand—perhaps the last great moving in the world's history. There are encouraging signs—the Jesus movement among American youth, revivals on Christian college campuses, unprecedented evangelical publishing, fantastic Pentecostal growth in Latin America, revival in Indonesia and some parts of Africa, new openness to the Gospel among Hindus in India, new and persuasive voices in evangelical theology. It may indeed be the world is coming of age in the most profound sense—coming to recognize its utter need for a sure word from the living God. Prophecies such as Joel 2:28-32 were not exhausted on the Day of Pentecost."[13]

The passage in Joel speaks of the final Pentecost which will come just before Christ returns. Baptist minister Don Hawkinson said, "I sense we are on the verge of something big,"[14] and others have expressed the same feeling. Is it truly the last generation in which the final

FINAL EVENTS ON PLANET EARTH

Pentecost is already quickly spreading over the world in the fast-growing charismatic movement? Is this the great revival which will usher in the eternal kingdom, the great moving of God to conclude the gospel to the world?

Those who have carefully analyzed the charismatic movement have discovered that the emphases upon personal experience rather than upon God's Revealed Word, upon subjective evidences such as healing and speaking in tongues instead of upon a "Thus saith the Lord," earmark it as a counterfeit. But should we expect such a counterfeit on such an unprecedented scale?

Ellen G. White clearly states, "Notwithstanding the widespread declension of faith and piety, there are true followers of Christ in these churches. Before the final visitation of God's judgments upon the earth there will be among the people of the Lord such a revival of primitive godliness as has not been witnessed since apostolic times. The Spirit and power of God will be poured out upon His children. At that time many will separate themselves from those churches in which the love of this world has supplanted love for God and His word. Many, both of ministers and people, will gladly accept those great truths which God has caused to be proclaimed at this time to prepare a people for the Lord's second coming. The enemy of souls desires to hinder this work; and *before* the time for such a movement shall come, he will endeavor to prevent it by introducing a *counterfeit*. In those churches which he can bring under his deceptive power he will make it appear that God's special blessing is poured out; there will

CHARISMATIC MOVEMENT?

be manifest what is thought to be great religious interest. Multitudes will exult that God is working marvelously for them, when the work is that of another spirit. Under a religious guise, Satan will seek to extend his influence over the Christian world."[15]

If the counterfeit comes just prior to the genuine, and if the charismatic movement is the predicted counterfeit (as many believe it to be), then the genuine Pentecost is imminent.

The strategy of Satan is subtle. Get the masses to look anywhere for authority other than the Bible. Siren voices call out, "Look within," "Cling to tongues," "Trust in the Spirit's baptism." But it's the same voice that booms out in rock beat, the same voice that calls, "C'mon, the crime show on TV is just entertainment." It is Satan's plan to seduce man from the safety of God's control in order to dominate and destroy him. His scheme transcends national and religious barriers. Charismatics go for a "religious high" that launches them way beyond the safe confines of objective truth. Blind to the emotional similarity exhibited in heathen cults, they do not realize that Satan is bringing the whole world under his sway. As *Christianity Today* pointed out, "Many Christians in the charismatic movement are insulated by the comparison often made between their spiritual experiences and parallel phenomena in non-Christian religions. Yet these believers need to be especially aware of the wiles of the devil in infiltration and counterfeiting."[16]

---

[1] *Eternity,* January, 1975, p. 11.

FINAL EVENTS ON PLANET EARTH

[2]*Sunday,* July-August, 1973, p. 3.

[3]*The Common Catechism, a Book of Christian Faith* (New York: Seabury Press, 1975). See *Newsweek*, March 24, 1975, pp. 64, 65.

[4]*Christianity Today,* June 23, 1972, p. 34.

[5]"Religious News Service," April 11, 1973.

[6]*Review and Herald,* October 26, 1972, p. 11.

[7]*Ibid.,* April 26, 1973, p. 12.

[8]*Christianity Today,* April 13, 1973, p. 55.

[9]*Ibid.,* June 23, 1972, p. 35.

[10]*Time,* October 8, 1973, p. 102.

[11]*Christianity Today,* September 15, 1972, p. 50.

[12]*Ibid.,* pp. 50, 51.

[13]*Ibid.,* January 7, 1972, p. 12.

[14]*Ibid.,* March 3, 1972, p. 37.

[15]*The Great Controversy,* p. 464, emphasis supplied.

[16]*Christianity Today,* an editorial "The Reality of Demons," December 8, 1972, p. 30.

CHARISMATIC MOVEMENT?

Chapter 10

Why the Rise
of the Occult?

Have you ever heard the ancient legend of the magical tower with a prophetic mirror on top? Apparently originating in India, the story tells of a magician who built a high edifice housing a mirror which showed all the town. When enemy soldiers marched toward the town, while yet a great distance away the mirror detected them like radar does today and pictured them appearing on something like a TV screen, thus warning the inhabitants.

The legend spread to many countries, taking on a variety of forms. In Rhodes the mirror, hung on the neck of their Colossus, revealed the ships that sailed to Syria and Egypt. The tower mirror in Alexandria exposed hostile vessels from Greece or the west while they were still fifty sailing days away from the city. So the stories go. The mirror in the legends represents an early form of crystal gazing.[1]

From time immemorial curious or frightened men have attempted to peer into the future—sometimes through crystal balls, a glass, or in the transparency of water. *Scrying* is the name given to seeing visions (like faces or an approaching enemy) in a smooth surface. Water is a favored element for scrying. Cylicomancy, gastromancy, hydromancy, lecanomancy, and pegomancy are five types of water scrying. Crystal gazing is crystallomancy, stone scrying is lithomancy, and using the fingernails of an unpolluted boy for divination the occultists call onychomancy. Mirror gazing atop ancient towers is called catoptromancy, or enoptromancy.

"Man is today undergoing a period of drastic change. A new world has suddenly dawned upon him which he had not the foresight to prepare for."[2] So wrote Arthur Lyons in the chapter "It's Later Than You Think." The new world is an occult-filled one.

"General occult phenomena and esoteric religion have become the 'in' thing in America."[3] For example, as Morris Cerullo reported, "There is enough business to keep 10,000 full-time and 175,000 part-time astrologers working. An estimated 40 million Americans aided by 10,000 professional astrologers have turned the zodiac following into a $200,000,000 a year business. Currently there are several computers engaged in casting and interpreting horoscopes. One of these prints out a 10,000-word horoscope in minutes for about $20. Another provides horoscopes twenty-four hours a day on about 2,000 campuses in America. A third is located in Grand Central Station in New York City, printing out about 500 horoscopes a day."[4]

Astrological horoscopes constitute today's most popular crystal balls. Millions around the world consult the papers to get insight into that day.

FINAL EVENTS ON PLANET EARTH

The newspaper is today's tower, and the horoscope the mirror. A new world indeed—but really as ancient as the hoary legend from India.

Around the world some two hundred different occult practices exist, of which people in America engage in seventy-five of them.[5] The Ouija board is one form. Patented in 1892 by William Fuld, it had sluggish sales, but in 1969 the *Wall Street Journal* estimated a grand sale of two million boards. Now it is more popular than Monopoly.[6]

Occult book sales boom. Doubleday's recently formed Universe Book Club exploded into 100,000 membership in only two years. Its speciality is the occult.[7] San Francisco's Anton LaVey's *Satanic Bible* is outselling the Holy Bible two to one; and in bookstores near college campuses it has been known to outsell the Bible one hundred to one.[8] Nearly ten million witches practice in America. Morris Cerullo claims that "witchcraft classes are being taught in many high schools from California to New York under a variety of titles ranging from 'Literature of the Supernatural' to 'History of the Occult.' High school newspapers across the country have been running an increasing number of features on witchcraft, frequently glorifying it."[9]

Eastern mystic religions flaunt their wares in the open market of so-called Christian countries. Watered-down Christianity has created a vacuum filled by Buddhism and Hinduism from the Orient. Emil Brunner threw out Biblical authority, Joseph Fletcher jettisoned absolutes, and Bishop John Robinson and Rudolf Bultmann torpedoed faith in the Second Advent. The British Beatles turned to

WHY THE RISE OF THE OCCULT?

Indian religion and meditation, and hordes of youth followed. Now "Eastern mysticism has become a fad among the youth and much of the jet set."[10]

We could mention numerous other forms of the occult such as scientology—headed by L. Ron Hubbard, which claims a world membership of fifteen million—white and black magic, interest in ESP, and clairvoyance. But the manifold forms of the occult have but one purpose—to control human beings. As Arthur Lyons put it, "Satanism is primarily a religion, for it seeks as a goal the surrender of self in the most extreme tradition of religion."[11] Satan is making his final bid to take over the world, and the occult is one chosen medium through which he seeks to accomplish it.

Kardecism offers a good example of Satan's take-over bid. It is a religion of the occult in Brazil started by French professor Denizard Hippolyte-Leon Rivail. One of Satan's spirits informed the professor that in another life (reincarnation) he was Allan Kardec; so the Frenchman accepted his allegedly old name in place of his present one. As the spirits communicated with him, Kardec affirmed, "The time has come . . . for the teaching of Christ to be complemented and for science to unveil some of the meanings which He purposely left occult."[12]

When Kardec first heard of moving tables, he dismissed the report as contrary to nature. But he later admitted that "one night in May, 1855, at the home of Madame Plaine Maison, I myself witnessed the phenomenon of tables cirling around, jumping and even running as it were,

FINAL EVENTS ON PLANET EARTH

in such conditions that any doubts were dispelled. That was a fact; there must be a cause, I thought."[13] "I thought that in these obscure and controversial phenomena could be the key to the problem of the past and future of humanity."[14] Kardec wanted that key to the future. He faced the ancient tower mirror in another form.

For two years Kardec asked questions of the spirit and received answers. He published 1,018 of them in his book *The Book of the Spirits* (1857). The questions ranged from Creation to the coming future. Other books followed such as *The Book of Medicines* and *The Gospels as Interpreted by Spiritism.*

One of his releases people today call the Bible of Kardecism. In fact, 160 miles from the plush, ultramodern new capital of Brasilia lies Polemero, a spiritist city. It boasts a noncrime record. How? "We all read Kardec's gospels, and no one thinks of committing a crime."[15] Millions in Brazil follow Kardecism. It seems to be good, but it is one medium through which Satan works to control the masses.

One unusual type of occult influence has appeared in the life of the near illiterate Francisco Candido Xavier who has published seventy-nine books. Francisco, or Chico as friends call him, is possessed by another spirit. When it overpowers him, his hand flies across the paper, writing at a speed impossible in ordinary life. In 1932 he published *Parnassus Beyond the Grave,* a new book of poetry with fifty-six different contributors—all dead. It includes the great poets of Portugal and Brazil such as Guerra Junqueiro, Antero de

WHY THE RISE OF THE OCCULT?

Quental, Augusto dos Anjos, and Castro Alves. The book duplicates exactly the varying styles and themes of each poet. Spirits can accurately reproduce another's literary style.

In 1939 Chico found himself face-to-face with Agrippino Grieco, one of Brazil's leading literary critics. A packed hall looked on in suspense as someone handed empty sheets of paper to Grieco for his signature—to avoid any fakery—and then Chico began writing on them with furious speed. New poems from great writers long dead, such as Augusto dos Anjos and Humberto de Compas, filled the papers, each with the precise literary skills, nuances, and historical references that an expert looks for in the works of the masters. Critic Grieco read them in stunned amazement.

In 1943 Chico made available *New Stories From Beyond the Grave,* allegedly by dead Humberto de Compas. While alive, Compas never sold more than 20,000 of any of his books, but the supposedly posthumous book of his sold 150,000 copies, or seven and one half times as many.

The spirit guide for Chico calls himself Immanuel. He has dictated to Chico on virtually every passage in the New Testament and predicted that the present form of the world will end by the year 2000.[16]

The occult is one avenue through which Satan seeks to control mankind, and it is attracting the masses as never before. It is even sweeping the so-called Christian countries. Ellen G. White declared, "As we near the close of time, there will be greater and still greater external parade of heathen power; heathen deities will manifest

FINAL EVENTS ON PLANET EARTH

their signal power, and will exhibit themselves before the cities of the world; and this delineation has already begun to be fulfilled."[17]

---

[1] Theodore Besterman, *Crystal Gazing* (New York: University Books Inc., 1965), pp. 9-12.

[2] Arthur Lyons, Jr., *The Second Coming, Satanism in America* (New York: Dodd, Mead and Co., 1970), p. 8.

[3] *Ibid.*, p. 10.

[4] Morris Cerullo, *The Back Side of Satan* (Illinois: Creation House, 1973), p. 13.

[5] *Ibid.*, p. 12.

[6] *Ibid.*, p. 13.

[7] *Ibid.*, p. 15.

[8] *Ibid.*, p. 18.

[9] *Ibid.*, p. 16.

[10] Lyons, *op. cit.*, p. 10.

[11] *Ibid.*, p. 16.

[12] Pedro McGregor and T. Stratton Smith, *Jesus of the Spirits* (New York: Stein and Day, 1967), p. 103.

[13] *Ibid.*, p. 109.

[14] *Ibid.*, p. 109.

[15] *Ibid.*, p. 102.

[16] *Ibid.*, pp. 120-130.

[17] Ellen G. White, *Testimonies to Ministers and Gospel Workers* (Mountain View, California: Pacific Press Publishing Association, 1944), pp. 117, 118.

WHY THE RISE OF THE OCCULT?

Chapter 11

How Dangerous Is Spiritualism?

The Ouija board lay on a small table in front of them. Huddled over it, Jane Roberts and her husband presented question after question and watched the hand turn to letters to spell out answers. Suddenly Jane became possessed by a person called Seth. "Write what I dictate to you. These are messages to be published." Pen and paper took the place of the Ouija board, and Jane began writing. Scores of sessions with the spirit resulted in 6,800 pages of material from the person alleged to be Seth. Prentice Hall published two books based on the spirit encounters.[1]

The 1970 book speaks of death. Seth says, "I can assure you that death is another beginning, and that when you are dead, you are not silenced. For is this voice that you now hear, silence? Is this presence that you sense within this room, death? ... The grave is not the end, for such a noisy one as I never spoke with the lips of death. . . . You have lived before and will live again, and when you are done with physical existence, you will still live."[2]

Thrust before Jane was the ancient lie—"Ye shall not surely die" (Genesis 3:4), and she believed it.

Time's cover story for November 13, 1972, talks about Richard Bach's book *Jonathan Livingston Seagull,* the best-selling fiction release of 1972, with close to two million copies purchased. Richard Bach admits that an audible voice dictated the book to him. It teaches that there is heaven and no death.[3]

Newsweek of July 12, 1976, reported on Dr. Elisabeth Kübler-Ross's work in thanatology (study of death). The "internationally respected expert on the psychiatric dimensions of dying now claims that she has proof that 'there is life after death.' "[4] Dr. Kübler-Ross has collected a number of experiences of people who nearly died but have been revived in time. The people believed that they had left their bodies and moved about, even seeing their own selves as dead and meeting deceased relatives and friends. Some experts view the experiences as a psychological accommodation to one's impending death, especially since the same thing happens both to those who do not believe in God and an afterlife and to those who do. Others, however, seize upon such stories as proof for the existence of an afterlife.

The above examples in different ways promote the idea that death is but a doorway into continued living. Many suppose that man, after all, is immortal. Death is just a delusion. It really begins the more abundant life. Such presuppositions make spiritualism creditable to those who do not know the real truth of the matter.

Did you know that spiritism is classified as a church and that its progress has been rapid? In 1848, modern spiritualism began in New York,

FINAL EVENTS ON PLANET EARTH

and yet only six years later it spread across every part of the United States, even pushed into Europe. By 1858 the first spiritualistic church group had organized itself in Michigan. The mediums practicing in America numbered some thirty thousand in 1864. And by the year 1880, only six years after the Seventh-day Adventist Church had sent J. N. Andrews (its first overseas missionary) to Europe, spiritualism had already extended over the world. Thus modern spiritualism, which began four years after the launching of our movement, raced us across the globe to claim a worldwide influence while we were only just beginning to reach out beyond North America.

By 1893 spiritualism, coming to be considered a church, initiated a program to convert the world. A year later it claimed 60 million adherents and published two hundred journals—an astounding accomplishment. In 1913 its adherents founded the Progressive Spiritual Church to establish spiritualism on a more religious basis. It is interesting to note that the *Encyclopedia Americana* defines spiritualism as "a religious sect or denomination, a form of Christianity."[5]

Of spiritualism's swift growth, Ellen G. White wrote, "I saw the rapidity with which this delusion was spreading. A train of cars was shown me, going with the speed of lightning. The angel bade me look carefully. I fixed my eyes upon the train. It seemed that the whole world was on board. Then he showed me the conductor, a fair, stately person, whom all the passengers looked up to and reverenced. I was perplexed and asked my attending angel who it was. He said, 'It is Satan. He is

HOW DANGEROUS IS SPIRITUALISM?

the conductor, in the form of an angel of light. He has taken the world captive. They are given over to strong delusions, to believe a lie that they may be damned. His agent, the highest in order next to him, is the engineer, and others of his agents are employed in different offices as he may need them, and they are all going with lightning speed to perdition.' "[6]

And in reference to spiritualism's attempt to make itself appear Christian, Ellen White said, "It is true that spiritualism is now changing its form and, veiling some of its more objectionable features, is assuming a Christian guise."[7] "As spiritualism more closely imitates the nominal Christianity of the day, it has greater power to deceive and ensnare. Satan himself is converted, after the modern order of things. . . . Through the agency of spiritualism, miracles will be wrought, the sick will be healed, and many undeniable wonders will be performed. And as the spirits will profess faith in the Bible, and manifest respect for the institutions of the church, their work will be accepted as a manifestation of divine power."[8]

Spiritualism is out to wreck Christianity. It has donned a Christian appearance only to deal the deathblow. We live in an "age of guise." Just as the tempter spoke through the most beautiful animal (the serpent) in Eden, so he has created his own church to torpedo Christianity. Through it he will prepare the world to accept his ultimate delusion—appearing as Christ in dazzling brightness.

Spiritualism's *Centennial Book,* page 50, ex-

FINAL EVENTS ON PLANET EARTH

poses the plan in part. Spiritualism "is destined to transform, if not, perhaps, in time, do away with, theology, which has been maintained by a hierarchy, and to make *the life of the Spirit* the all in all in religion, as it was the all in all with the founder of Christianity." According to this book, Jesus taught that "salvation comes from *within,* not from without. There could be no such thing, in the nature of things, as a vicarious atonement for the sins of the world. Man can be *at one* with the Universal Spirit only through his own spiritual vitality. That alone is Salvation."[9]

The attack is obviously against Christ. It declares that man doesn't need a Saviour; salvation comes from within, from man, not from Christ. It thrusts man back upon his own supposed resources, away from the only Saviour who can help him. "Satan is making the world believe that the Bible is a mere fiction, or at least a book suited to the infancy of the race, but now to be lightly regarded, or cast aside as obsolete. And to take the place of the word of God he holds out spiritual manifestations. Here is a channel wholly under his *control;* by this means he can make the world believe what he will."[10]

Under spiritualism man feels self-sufficient. And the moment he believes that he does not need a Saviour, he falls under the control of Satan.

In fact, spiritualism bills itself as the next world religion. Its *Centennial Book* states, "Spiritualism is the coming universal religion. It is the life blood of Christianity; in fact, it is Christianity plus."[11] The *Spiritualist Manual* claims, "It is the mission of spiritualism to revolutionize the world,

HOW DANGEROUS IS SPIRITUALISM?

to sweep away the accumulated rubbish of centuries of ignorance and superstition."[12]

Ellen G. White sees the "sweeping" action quite differently. "Church members love what the world loves and are ready to join with them [ungodly people], and Satan determines to unite them in one body and thus strengthen his cause by sweeping them all into the ranks of spiritism."[13]

In chapter 9 we looked at the charismatic movement, which is fast uniting the churches. Could it be that spiritualism is the power behind that phenomenon? Both the charismatic movement and spiritualism have grown rapidly, appear to be Christian, perform miracles, and unite the different elements in the world as nothing else has been able to do.

"According to a 1968 Gallup poll, fully 73 percent of all Americans believe in some kind of life after death. And another Gallup survey last year found that 98 percent of Roman Catholic priests, 86 percent of Protestant ministers, and 68 percent of rabbis believe that 'souls live on after death.' "[14]

Given such a background, America—as indeed it is true for the rest of the world—is ripe for the thrust foretold in Revelation 6:13, 14, KJV. "And I saw three unclean spirits like frogs come out of the mouth of the dragon, and out of the mouth of the beast, and out of the mouth of the false prophet. For they are the spirits of devils, working miracles, which go forth unto the kings of the earth and of the whole world, to gather them to the battle of the great day of God Almighty." Spiritualism will help array the whole

FINAL EVENTS ON PLANET EARTH

world against Christ and His remnant.

The following message from the spirit named Seth shows spiritualism's anti-Christ nature. "Christ, the historical Christ, was not crucified. . . . He had no intention of dying in that manner. . . . Christ did not take part in it. There was a conspiracy. . . . The man chosen was drugged—hence the necessity of helping him carry the cross (see Luke 23)—and he was told that he was Christ. . . . The tomb was empty because this same group carted the body away. . . . Christ was a great psychic. He caused the wounds to appear then (Easter morning before Mary Magdalene) upon His own body. . . . Peter three times denied the Lord (Matthew 26), saying he did not know Him, because he recognized that the person was not Christ. . . . He (Christ) knew that without wounds they would not believe He was Christ Himself, because they were so convinced that He died with those wounds (see John 20). They were to be a method of identification, to be dispensed with when He explained the true circumstances. . . . (Judas was in on the plot, and pointed out the drugged impersonator to the mob in Gethsemane.) He knew of the conspiracy, and feared that the real Christ would be captured. Therefore he handed over to the authorities a man known to be the self-styled messiah—to save, not to destroy, the life of the historical Christ." [15]

What a travesty of the facts! The best way to expose such a cynical counterfeit is to remove its foundation—the false "state of the dead" belief. In recent years a growing number of reputable scholars have questioned what the churches

HOW DANGEROUS IS SPIRITUALISM?

commonly teach on the subject. French theologian Oscar Cullmann leveled it as Greek philosophy.[16]

Swiss theologian Karl Barth called for a total view of man as a body and soul that do not separate. In his *Church Dogmatics* he speaks of a besouled body and bodily-soul to communicate its integral unity. American theologian Krister Stendahl, dean of Harvard's Divinity School, rejects the idea of natural immortality.[17] The Bible truth on the condition of the dead is our only safety against spiritualism.

"Satan has long been preparing for his final effort to deceive the world. The foundation of his work was laid by the assurance given to Eve in Eden: 'Ye shall not surely die.' 'In the day ye eat thereof, then your eyes shall be opened, and ye shall be as gods, knowing good and evil.' Little by little he has prepared the way for his master-piece of deception in the development of spiritualism."[18] Spiritualism is one of his means to control humanity.

In mercy God has warned us, "The experience of the past will be repeated. In the future, Satan's superstitions will assume new forms. Errors will be presented in a pleasing and a flattering manner. False theories, clothed with garments of light, will be presented to God's people. Thus Satan will try to deceive, if possible, the very elect. Most seducing influences will be exerted; minds will be hypnotized."[19]

---

[1]*The Seth Material,* 1970; and *Seth Speaks: The Eternal Validity of the Soul,* 1972. The scene is reconstructed, based on the Ouija board contacts with the spirit world which led to possession by Seth.

FINAL EVENTS ON PLANET EARTH

[2]*The Seth Material,* pp. 2-4.

[3]*Time,* November 13, 1972, see pp. 60-66.

[4]*Newsweek,* July 12, 1976, p. 41.

[5]*Encyclopedia Americana* (Americana Corporation, New York, 1969), Vol. 25, p. 421.

[6]*Early Writings,* p. 263.

[7]*The Great Controversy,* p. 558.

[8]*Ibid.,* p. 588.

[9]*Spiritualism's Centennial Book,* p. 50, quoted in Leroy Edwin Froom's *Spiritualism Today,* p. 23.

[10]*The Great Controversy,* p. 557 (emphasis supplied).

[11]*Spiritualism's Centennial Book,* p. 69, quoted in *Spiritualism Today,* p. 17.

[12]*Spiritualist Manual,* p. 79, quoted in Roy Allan Anderson's *Secrets of the Spirit World,* p. 44.

[13]*The Great Controversy,* p. 588.

[14]*Newsweek,* April 3, 1972, p. 58.

[15]*As Seth Speaks,* pp. 435-437.

[16] Oscar Cullmann, *Immortality of the Soul or Resurrection of the Dead* (New York: The Macmillan Company, 1958), pp. 16-18.

[17]*Newsweek,* April 3, 1972, p. 58.

[18]*The Great Controversy,* p. 561.

[19]*Testimonies for the Church,* Vol. 8, p. 293.

HOW DANGEROUS IS SPIRITUALISM?

Chapter 12

What About Miracles?

They carried her into the home like a load of fragile glass. Body shrunken and twisted by painful rheumatoid arthritis, sixty-six-year-old Betty Kmieciak wondered what Rev. John Scudder could do for her hopeless case. Placed on a bed in the minister's home outside Chicago, she looked up to the healer bending over her.

"Relax and be filled with the healing power of God," he spoke soothingly. Mrs. Kmieciak felt herself sinking into semiconsciousness. Scudder applied his healing powers for forty-five minutes, then placed one bony finger on the aged woman's forehead and another on her solar plexus. "You are filled with warmth, you are in a glow," he whispered, and waited to see her reaction. She blinked, grabbed her cane, and walked for the first time in almost two years.[1]

Ours is the age of the miraculous. In fact, as *Newsweek* reported, "the demand for psychic healing is spreading like wildfire, rapidly outdistancing the supply of the healers."[2] Even in an era given over to sports, healing has pushed aside scheduled matches. For example, Jacques Girard stormed the capital of the Ivory Coast with his miracle-ministry. Thirty thousand people packed the Champroux Stadium, forcing cancellation of sporting events for a further five nights beyond the agreed slate of meetings.[3]

Miracles have become the new authority of the day. Churches split asunder by theology now seem destined to be joined through the miraculous. "Papists, who boast of miracles as a certain sign of the true church, will be readily deceived by this wonder-working power; and Protestants, having cast away the shield of truth, will also be deluded. Papists, Protestants, and worldlings will alike accept the form of godliness without the power."[4]

A miracle can override even arguments against such things as tongues speaking. One healed man affirmed, " 'When Ken prayed for me, he prayed in a beautiful language I had never heard before. You might have intellectual arguments against the baptism of the Holy Spirit and speaking in tongues, but when somebody prays for you in tongues and heals you, what is there left to argue about? That was the first time I had heard someone manifesting a new language.' "[5] The healing threw out intellectual questions and shoved doctrine aside.

Miracles can convince even a medical scientist. Dr. Richard O'Wellen, an assistant professor of medicine at Johns Hopkins University, followed the late Kathryn Kuhlman for over a decade since she "cured" his daughter of a congenitally dislocated hip. In utter amazement he blurted out, "I can't explain it, and I can't understand it, but it has to be God."[6]

"It has to be God." Because it gets results, the

FINAL EVENTS ON PLANET EARTH

new authority and not doctrines is the ultimate evidence for the genuine. Miracles bring their own credentials. But do they?

What supremacy do miracles carry anyway? After all, they also take place outside the Christian world. As in the case of charismatic phenomena (Chapter 9), so miracles also transcend denominations and religions. They occur as comfortably in African witch-doctor magic as in American charismatic healing services. How, then, can they serve as credentials for true religion? Can all religions be right, even though diametrically opposed? How can opposites be true—even substantiated by the same miraculous event? Obviously we confront a dilemma, one that miracle proponents have not faced up to.

Jesus appealed to His works as evidence of His divinity. "The same works that I do, bear witness of me, that the Father hath sent me" (John 5:36, KJV). Several times Christ emphasized the point (John 10:25, 37, 38). The observers likewise saw in His miracles evidence that He was the One to believe in. In fact, "many believed in his name, when they saw the miracles which he did" (John 2:23, KJV). Several similar statements appear in the Gospel (John 3:2; 6:14; 11:45, 47, 48, 53; 12:10, 11).

But the Bible clearly indicates charlatans will attempt to copy Christ's genuine methods: "For there shall arise false Christs, and false prophets, and shall shew great signs and wonders; insomuch that, if it were possible, they shall deceive the very elect" (Matthew 24:24, KJV).

Now suppose someone comes to town wanting

WHAT ABOUT MIRACLES?

to prove that God still lives. The crowds gather, and you find yourself at the fringe looking on. The man, center stage, claims that the time for Elijah has come. Soon Jesus will return. Your heart beats with joy to hear such a message.

The Elijah test, you recall, involved fire from heaven: "And the God who answers by fire, he is God" (1 Kings 18:24, RSV). A long, hot, bloody day on Mt. Carmel produced nothing at the hands of the Baal priests, but the God of heaven answered by fire, and Elijah's Lord routed the false gods (verses 38-41). Now you wait expectantly. Suddenly fire descends and the crowd falls to its knees. "This is the great power of God. Hallelujah! Listen to His message." Will you listen and obey? Will the words be authoritative because backed up by the Elijah miracle?

The Bible says that in the last days Satan "doeth great wonders, so that he maketh fire come down from heaven on the earth in the sight of men, and deceiveth them that dwell on the earth by the means of those miracles which he had power to do in the sight of the beast; saying to them that dwell on the earth, that they should make an image to the beast, which had the wound by a sword, and did live" (Revelation 13:13, 14, KJV).

"You know that Satan will come in to deceive if possible the very elect. He claims to be Christ, and he is coming in, pretending to be the great medical missionary. He will cause fire to come down from heaven in the sight of men, to prove that he is God. We must stand barricaded by the truths of the Bible. The canopy of truth is the only canopy under which we can stand safely." [7]

FINAL EVENTS ON PLANET EARTH

We may expect a false Mt. Carmel test before Christ's return, a counterfeit of the genuine one of millennia ago.

A twofold strategy will arise: (1) Satan will make it seem that miracles have occurred. "God's Word declares that Satan will work miracles. He will make people sick, and then will suddenly remove from them his satanic power. They will then be regarded as healed. These works of apparent healing will bring Seventh-day Adventists to the test."[8] (2) He will also perform real miracles. " 'He doeth great wonders, so that he maketh fire come down from heaven on the earth in the sight of men, and deceiveth them that dwell on the earth by the means of those miracles which he had power to do' (Revelation 13:13, 14, KJV). No mere impostures are here foretold. Men are deceived by the miracles which Satan's agents have power to do, not which they pretend to do."[9] Whether apparent or real, the strategy to deceive and control is the same.

And great will be the deception. His target is the entire world. "The enemy is preparing to deceive the whole world by his miracle-working power."[10] The Bible says, "I saw three unclean spirits like frogs come out of the mouth of the dragon, and out of the mouth of the beast, and out of the mouth of the false prophet. For they are the spirits of devils, working miracles, which go forth unto the kings of the earth and of the whole world, to gather them to the battle of that great day of God Almighty" (Revelation 16:13, 14, KJV).

Why do we not see so many genuine miracles today as in Christ's time? "The way in which

WHAT ABOUT MIRACLES?

Christ worked was to preach the Word, and to relieve suffering by miraculous works of healing. But I am instructed that we cannot now work in this way, for Satan will exercise his power by working miracles. God's servants today could not work by means of miracles, because spurious works of healing, claiming to be divine, will be wrought." [11]

But a new day is imminent. A change is coming. Miracles have a part in the finale. For "servants of God, with their faces lighted up and shining with holy consecration, will hasten from place to place to proclaim the message from heaven. By thousands of voices, all over the earth, the warning will be given. Miracles will be wrought, the sick will be healed, and signs and wonders will follow the believers." [12]

But God's people will not do such miracles just to prove a point. Suppose you have just preached a powerful sermon on the Sabbath. You have spoken on the joys of observing the right day and urged the hearers to accept God's seventh day of rest. Then someone shouts out, "My minister keeps Sunday, and I believe he is right because he works miracles. If your day is the right one, heal this sick man. Show us a miracle. Prove yourself." All eyes fasten on you. You are on the spot. What will you do?

"Unbelievers will require them to do some miracle, if they believe God's special power is in the church, and that they are the chosen people of God. Unbelievers, who are afflicted with infirmities, will require them to work a miracle upon them, if God is with them. Christ's followers

FINAL EVENTS ON PLANET EARTH

should imitate the example of their Lord. Jesus, with His divine power, did not do any mighty works for Satan's diversion. Neither can the servants of Christ. They should refer the unbelieving to the written, inspired testimony for evidence of their being the loyal people of God, and heirs of salvation." [13] "If they will not be convinced by inspired testimony, a manifestation of God's power would not benefit them." [14]

Perhaps Matthew 7:22, 23 records the greatest tragedy: "Many will say to me in that day, Lord, Lord, have we not prophesied in thy name? and in thy name have cast out devils? and in thy name done many wonderful works? And then will I profess unto them, I never knew you: depart from me, ye that work iniquity."

Imagine—the very miracles thought to evidence the genuine will stand revealed as the works of falsehood. "The last great delusion is soon to open before us. Antichrist is to perform his marvelous works in our sight. So closely will the counterfeit resemble the true that it will be impossible to distinguish between them except by the Holy Scriptures. By their testimony every statement and every miracle must be tested." [15]

Tremendous encouragement awaits the Bible student, however. Satan cannot "hold under his power one soul who honestly desires, at whatever cost, to know the truth." [16] Remember that "the Bible will never be superseded by miraculous manifestations." [17] The question then is, Are the people of God now so firmly established upon His Word that they would not yield to the evidence of their senses? Would they, in such a crisis, cling to

WHAT ABOUT MIRACLES?

the Bible and the Bible only?[18]

Our calling is to proclaim the Bible, not to perform miracles. Like John the Baptist, we are to prepare the way for the Lord. John, we read, "did no miracle" (John 10:41, KJV). True, he went forth in the spirit and power of Elijah (Luke 1:17), as we must, but the message rather than miracles was his burden, and it is ours. John represents our church.[19]

"Behold the Lamb of God"—not, "Behold the miracle." In a generation that has jettisoned the Bible as mere excess baggage on the pilgrimage of life, Seventh-day Adventists believe "that which is greater than all miracles"—"a firm reliance upon a 'thus saith the Lord.' "[20] It speaks of the greatest miracle of all—a transformed life under the control of God.

[1]*Newsweek,* April 29, 1974, p. 67.

[2]*Ibid.*

[3]*British Advent Messenger,* July 26, 1974.

[4]*The Great Controversy,* p. 588.

[5]*The Voice,* Full Gospel Business Men's Fellowship International Publication, July-August, 1972.

[6]*Newsweek,* April 29, 1974, p. 67.

[7]Ellen G. White, *Medical Ministry* (Mountain View, California: Pacific Press Publishing Association, 1932), pp. 87, 88.

[8]Ellen G. White, *Selected Messages* (Washington, D.C.: Review and Herald Publishing Association, 1958), Book Two, p. 53.

[9]*The Great Controversy,* p. 553.

[10]*Selected Messages,* Book Two, p. 96.

[11]*Ibid.,* p. 54.

[12]*The Great Controversy,* p. 612.

[13]Ellen G. White, *Spiritual Gifts* (Washington, D.C.: Review and Herald Publishing Association, 1945 facsimile reprint), Vol. IV, p. 151.

[14]*Ibid.,* p. 150.

FINAL EVENTS ON PLANET EARTH

[15]*The Great Controversy,* p. 593.
[16]*Ibid.,* p. 528.
[17]*Selected Messages,* Book Two, p. 48.
[18]*The Great Controversy,* p. 593.
[19]*Early Writings,* p. 155.
[20]Ellen G. White, *Review and Herald,* May 14, 1908, p. 8.

WHAT ABOUT MIRACLES?

Chapter 13

Why the
Time of Trouble?

"At 6:40 PM last September 20, in suburban Miami, a fusillade of bullets splintered the doorway to the Upthegrove family's heavy-construction business. 'Oh, . . . don't move, anybody!' screamed office manager, Yvonne Upthegrove. Under fire were her husband, Lingo, and his brother Howard.

"The family had been victims of a campaign of terror for nearly a year, ever since setting up their operation independent of the Union. On Thanksgiving Day, 1971, the brakes of a huge crane were mysteriously tampered with, and its 3,000-pound boom dropped 30 feet, fracturing Lingo's skull. He was unconscious for a week. Next month the boom fell again, requiring costly repairs. Someone had poured acid on its brake bands. One incident followed another. Shortly after the family borrowed to buy a used $85,000 track crane, a grinding compound was poured into one of its engines. Damage, nearly $6,000. The same thing was done to the firm's floating pile driver. Another crane was firebombed and a security guard's car burned up. Threatening phone calls had come night after night." [1]

Ellen G. White wrote that "the trades unions will be one of the agencies that will bring upon this earth a time of trouble such as has not been since the world began."[2] "These unions are one of the signs of the last days. Men are binding up in bundles ready to be burned. . . . Thou shalt love the Lord . . . and thy neighbor as thyself. . . . How can men obey these words, and at the same time pledge themselves to support that which deprives their neighbors of freedom of action?"[3]

The *Register,* of Napa, California, reports that "strikes and shop floor militancy are on the up all over the world. Days lost in the forty-six countries that submit regular returns to the International Labor Organization in Geneva have more than doubled from an annual average of 68 million in the five years, 1963-67, to 126 million in 1968-72."[4]

Satan surges forth to dominate the world. Through TV carnage, mass media, music, the charismatic movement, spiritualism, and labor unions he seeks in different ways to accomplish the same end. The Bible warns, "Woe to you, O earth and sea, for the devil has come down to you in great wrath, because he knows that his time is short!" (Revelation 12:12, RSV). "The wrath of Satan increases as his time grows short, and his work of deceit and destruction will reach its culmination in the time of trouble."[5] His whole strategy centers around destruction.

Another avenue Satan works through is natural calamities. "In accidents and calamities by sea and by land, in great conflagrations, in fierce tornadoes and terrific hailstorms, in tempests,

FINAL EVENTS ON PLANET EARTH

floods, cyclones, tidal waves, and earthquakes, in every place and in a thousand forms, Satan is exercising his power. He sweeps away the ripening harvest, and famine and distress follow. He imparts to the air a deadly taint, and thousands perish by the pestilence. These visitations are to become more and more frequent and disastrous."[6]

Satan will unite the world under his control before Christ's return (Revelation 13:3). All of Satan's deceptive means are for destruction.

Unprecedented trouble will come. It is almost here. Already *Christianity Today* can say, "We live in a world currently dominated by Satan; . . . his evil spirits, myriads of them, . . . do his will" and "wreak havoc in the world."[7] But today angels of God hold back most of Satan's fury (Revelation 7:1). Think what it will be like when they let go! The Scriptures state, "At that time shall arise Michael, the great prince who has charge of your people. And there shall be a time of trouble, such as never has been since there was a nation till that time" (Daniel 12:1, RSV).

"The restraint which has been upon the wicked is removed, and Satan has entire control of the finally impenitent. God's long-suffering has ended. . . . Satan will then plunge the inhabitants of the earth into one great, final trouble. . . . A single angel destroyed all the firstborn of the Egyptians and filled the land with mourning. When David offended against God by numbering the people, one angel caused that terrible destruction by which his sin was punished. The same destructive power exercised by holy angels when God commands will be exercised by evil angels when He

WHY THE TIME OF TROUBLE?

permits. There are forces now ready, and only waiting the divine permission, to spread desolation everywhere."[8]

Such is the broad context for natural disasters. They form a part of Satan's overall strategy to dominate and ruin. Actually such calamities are anything but natural—they are supernatural assaults on humanity—an exposure of the type of tyrant Satan is. But here we come to a puzzling question which we will pursue in the rest of the chapter. Why does a God of love allow His people, who have completed their commission and are ready for translation, to remain in our world to suffer through the worst time it has ever witnessed? They cannot win another convert, for probation has closed. Prepared to meet Christ, they long to go home, but God says, "No—not yet." Instead they are plunged into affliction known as "Jacob's trouble"—their Gethsemane. "Thus saith the Lord; we have heard a voice of trembling, of fear, and not of peace. . . . All faces are turned into paleness. Alas! for that day is great, so that none is like it: it is even the time of Jacob's trouble" (Jeremiah 30:3-7).

With probation's passing, the wicked are ripe for destruction as well as the saints ready for translation. All humanity has reached an irreversible point. Why, then, keep them all alive in the worst trouble ever? Why does God not destroy the wicked and take His people to heaven?

The answer is simple. The approaching great time of suffering is Satan's ultimate exposure.[9] Satan will reveal his true colors. Today's temptations look as enticing as the first one in Eden, if

FINAL EVENTS ON PLANET EARTH

not more so. But the coming trouble will clearly demonstrate the motive to possess that lies behind the devil's actions. Man and the whole universe will see Satan—for the first time granted entire control—operate as leader of the world. And the utter mess he will make of it—the unspeakable carnage and devastation—will shake the globe to its roots. It will appear that the earth is spinning off course, totally out of control. The world will seem as doomed as a plane in a nose-dive. Satan, who has always wanted to be king of the world, even offered Jesus its kingdoms if He would worship him. He believes he could run the universe better than God. The postprobation period will be his chance to do "his thing."

But could he not rule over the wicked alone? Why have God's redeemed been subjected to such a usurper? Because they will show what kind of God the Creator is. Satan hates God's law. From Adam's day to the present time the issue in the great controversy has involved obedience.[10] "Satan will devise every possible means to break down this high standard of piety as one altogether too strict."[11] It is "Satan's claim that the law is unjust, and cannot be obeyed."[12]

In this way Satan questions God's justice—His ability to control His people. Has God made the law beyond man's reach—beyond His sustaining power to help man keep? "No, a thousand times No!" God "is able to keep you from falling, and to present you faultless before the presence of his glory with exceeding joy" (Jude 24, KJV). God's people, with Paul, exclaim, "I am crucified with Christ: nevertheless I live; yet not I, but Christ

WHY THE TIME OF TROUBLE?

liveth in me" (Galatians 2:20, KJV). They know that without Him they can do nothing (John 15:5). They know that He rightly lays "the glory of man in the dust," and does "for man that which it is not in his power to do for himself."[13] They know that Jesus is far more than a pattern to copy—He is primarily a Saviour to cling to. Only Christ's substitution gives them hope and victory. His substitution for them qualifies all else—past, present, and future.

God's people have always found victory in utter dependence on Christ alone. In fact, "some few in every generation from Adam resisted his [Satan's] every artifice and stood forth as noble representatives of what it was in the power of man to do and to be—Christ working with human efforts, helping man in overcoming the power of Satan. Enoch and Elijah are the correct representatives of what the race might be through faith in Jesus Christ if they chose to be. Satan was greatly disturbed because these noble, holy men stood untainted amid the moral pollution surrounding them, perfected righteous characters, and were accounted worthy for translation to Heaven."[14] God has revealed the victorious freedom of His controlling presence in human lives throughout the centuries. Why then the postprobation period?

Contrary to Satan's charge, God is just. His control will bring victory to the final generation—in spite of the fact that they constitute the weakest in hereditary characteristics and the time they live in depicts the worst in satanic rule. Here is the Litmus test—the proof par excellence. If such men under such conditions will stand unmoved,

FINAL EVENTS ON PLANET EARTH

resting unruffled in the hands of Christ, then Satan's charge stands revealed as groundless. Such people offer incontrovertible evidence in favor of God. They show what God can do through yielded lives. The demonstration reveals God and not man. Men are merely the means through which He makes the revelation.

Weakened by a long history of sin, plunged into the most severe struggle of the ages, even they will be completely triumphant. What better proof could Christ have that the law is just, can be kept, because its standard is fair? Here is why God's people remain in the world to endure the final persecution. They are doing something to aid Christ, the One who has done everything to help them.

The time of trouble before the Second Advent will thus expose Satan for the tyrant he really is, and Christ will stand vindicated as the just Saviour. Two types of control will come into focus—the servile dictatorship of Satan and the gentle but magnetic leading of Jesus. The universe will see the devil as only bent on destruction but Christ as seeking to rescue from sin and annihilation.

And the final deliverance will be fantastic. Just as God preserved the three Hebrews in Nebuchadnezzar's furnace, for the Son of man stood there with them, so His people will survive through "Jacob's trouble" because Christ has promised, "Lo, I am with you alway, even unto the end of the world" (Matthew 28:20, KJV). They have nothing to fear. The weapons readied to kill them the wicked will actually use to slay their own leaders. The angry masses will go for blood, avenging their lost

WHY THE TIME OF TROUBLE?

condition on those who have deceived them. For the first time, albeit too late, they realize that God is with the small hated group.

Did you ever wonder why the Book of Revelation mentions the 144,000? They first appear in connection with the four angels' holding back the "winds of strife" (Revelation 7:1-4). God restrains total persecution long enough to allow the last generation of His people to settle into the truth both intellectually and spiritually so that nothing can move them. Can you see why God has waited so long? God's remnant people must be immovable before He releases the strife. To wait till the onrush of that fury will be too late. "None but those who have fortified the mind with the truths of the Bible will stand through the last great conflict." [15]

Even if only one sinned during the final trouble, the demonstration in behalf of God would be spoiled. To take a large number from different environments and backgrounds, and have each one stand unmoved, proves conclusively that—with God's help—one can obey the law.

Revelation 14:1-5 is the other passage which refers to the 144,000. It is significant that the passage introduces the "three angels' messages," our unique emphasis to the world. The two missions before the church are (1) to preach these messages to save men and (2) to form the 144,000 group to vindicate God's justice. Christ had the same double mission. He saved men and lived a perfect life to show that a created being who completely allows God to live out the law in him can overcome, thereby demonstrating God's jus-

FINAL EVENTS ON PLANET EARTH

tice and vindicating His name.

But because most Christians believe Christ had an advantage over other men, God will make it clear that even the last generation of men can be controlled by Him just as was Jesus. So Christ and the 144,000 stand together on Mount Zion (Revelation 14:1), and the group will always follow Christ wherever He goes throughout the universe in the coming kingdom (verse 5). Why? The 144,000 will sing the song of Moses and the Lamb, the song of their experience.[16] None but the 144,000 can sing it. Like Jesus, they will have come to the place of utter dependence upon God—in spite of all circumstances to the contrary. With every earthly support removed, they will cling to Him alone. "Jacob's trouble" will be their Gethsemane. Like Jesus, they will remain unmoved, under the complete and wonderful control of God.

The time of trouble should not be a horror to dread but a privilege to grasp. Those who go through that short time will be special exhibits forever—as those whom the Lord used to answer Satan's false charges—those totally controlled by God. No wonder Ellen G. White urges us, "Let us strive with all the power that God has given us to be among the hundred and forty-four thousand."[17]

The Upthegrove family stood alone with a whole union against them. Persecuted, they lost everything but their lives. But they remained unmoved, in control, and in a sense a symbol of the 144,000 who will face the whole world united against them—a globe welded together by the devil. Such unity is forming now, and given inter-

WHY THE TIME OF TROUBLE?

national turmoil, with the possibility of nuclear oblivion, the people of the world will gladly turn to the supposed Christ as Satan promises them peace if they will only get rid of the hated few who stubbornly keep God's Sabbath law. The latter's freedom will seemingly be gone. But if the righteous have in the present learned to stand for the truth despite everything, then they will not succumb during that worse crisis to come. They will show to the universe the freedom enjoyed under God's control and will thereby fulfill one vital purpose for the time of trouble.

---

[1]*Reader's Digest,* June, 1973.

[2]Ellen G.White, *Country Living* (Washington, D.C.: Review and Herald Publishing Association, 1946), p. 10.

[3]*Ibid.,* pp. 11, 12.

[4]*The Register,* Napa, California, October 23, 1974.

[5]*The Great Controversy,* p. 623.

[6]*Ibid.,* pp. 589, 590.

[7]*Christianity Today,* December 8, 1972.

[8]*The Great Controversy,* p. 614.

[9]From the viewpoint of eternity, the Crucifixion will be the ultimate exposure of Satan. But from the viewpoint of time, this postprobation period is the first chance he will have full control of the impenitent. His chaotic rule will constitute a self-exposure.

[10]*Patriarchs and Prophets* (Mountain View: Pacific Press Publishing Association, 1913), p. 73.

[11]Ellen G. White, *Child Guidance* (Washington, D.C.: Review and Herald Publishing Association, 1954), p. 80.

[12]Ellen G. White, *The Desire of Ages* (Mountain View: Pacific Press Publishing Association, 1913), p. 309.

[13]*Testimonies to Ministers,* p. 456.

[14]*Review and Herald,* March 3, 1874, p. 91.

[15]*The Great Controversy,* p. 593.

[16]*Ibid.,* p. 649.

[17]Ellen G. White comments, *SDA Bible Commentary* (Washington, D.C.: Review and Herald Publishing Association), Vol. 7, p. 970.

Chapter 14

What's Coming?

Gigantic waves pounded the ship, and it rolled like a top as the rough sea relentlessly rammed it. A crash, and the vessel shook violently. "Help! we're sinking!" scared men screamed above the roar. "Water's aboard the stern!" The ocean swirled into the aftermost cabins. "Brace the bulkheads!" someone shouted. Men rushed to reinforce them with heavy lumber. Wall after wall of water slammed the limping ship, shoving it about. The propeller shaft snapped. How long would those timbers hold? With bow rising high into the sky and stern sinking deep into the sea, the *Spree* floundered hopelessly.

Several days later, when all hope seemed gone, Dwight L. Moody tightly clutched a pole as the vessel reeled from side to side. He faced wide-eyed, pale-faced, anxious-looking people and read from Psalm 107 (here quoted from the Revised Standard Version): "They reeled and staggered like drunken men, and were at their wits' end. Then they cried to the Lord in their trouble, and he delivered them from their distress; he made the storm be still, and the waves of the sea were hushed. Then they were glad because they had quiet, and he brought

119

them to their desired haven" (verses 27-30).

After encouraging the frightened people, Moody went to his cabin and fell on his knees. He wrestled in prayer, longing for relief from the storm. Finally he committed the outcome to his Saviour, willing to die if it was Christ's will. Peace and calm came within, and sound sleep overtook him. Hours later excited voices awakened him at 3:00 AM. There, far out near the horizon, the lights of a steamer pierced the darkness. That distant ship, *Lake Huron,* later came to the *Spree* and towed it the long thousand miles to land and safety.

Satan, like a torpedo, seeks us out to shipwreck us from beneath or hurls storms along our pathway, circumstances designed to sink us. Anxiety, care, worry, doubt, and discouragement comprise some of the weapons he most effectively uses to accomplish his end. He knows that anxiety causes "great harm,"[1] tending "to break down the life forces,"[2] that worry encourages "weakness and disease,"[3] that doubt closes "the door to many blessings,"[4] that discouragement paralyzes faith and hope, making a person unfit for usefulness,[5] and that care diverts the mind from Christ.[6]

No one is immune. In fact, "into the experience of *all* there come times of keen disappointment and utter discouragement—days when sorrow is the portion, and it is hard to believe that God is still the kind benefactor of His earthborn children; days when troubles harass the soul, till death seems preferable to life."[7]

Consider Job, Elijah, and Jonah. The storms of life overwhelmed, engulfed, all three, and from out of the depths they cried to God to let them

FINAL EVENTS ON PLANET EARTH

die (Job 6:8-10; 1 Kings 19:4; Jonah 4:3). Others struggled to stay afloat. Joshua, faced with new leadership responsibilities, trembled with "great anxiety."[8] John the Baptist in prison battled doubt. "There were hours when the whispering of demons tortured his spirit, and the shadow of a terrible fear crept over him."[9] Paul, beset with perplexities and discouragements, exclaimed, "We were pressed out of measure, above strength, insomuch that we despaired even of life."[10]

Job, Elijah, Joshua, Jonah, John the Baptist, Paul—they were all good men, God's men—and yet the raging, relentless fury of life's storms battered them all for a time.

We live in a time of comparative peace. Angels still hold back strife (Revelation 7:3), but not forever. A typhoon is about to fling itself with full force upon the last generation of genuine Christians. Soon we will find ourselves in the middle of the final crisis.

How can we prepare for it? What is our ultimate hope for survival? What must we do to be saved? Forget the crisis—that is the best way to prepare for it! Astonishing? Yes, but true. Center your attention beyond it to Christ who is in control. When Peter did this, he walked on the sea, but when he dropped his gaze, he sank (Matthew 14:27-31).

Israelites dying of serpent bites in Edom gazed at the symbol of Jesus put up by Moses (see Numbers 21:6-9). When Elisha's servant trembled at Dothan because of the encircling army, God opened his eyes to behold the greater legions of God in control (see 2 Kings 6:11-17).

WHAT'S COMING?

Satan works to wrench the attention from above to focus it within. "Go, make the possessors of lands and money drunk with the cares of this life!"[11] "The Lord has shown me the danger of letting our minds be filled with worldly thoughts and cares. . . . If the mind is filled with other things, present truth is shut out, and there is no place in our foreheads for the seal of the living God."[12]

What about spiritual cares? I have found church members in different parts of the world concerned about their character development. We are called away from *all* cares, which includes worry about victory in your life, to the One who cares. The gospel is Christ—not the Christian, not me. It is freedom from self, even from self-improvement. Let us never forget it—the gospel is the Saviour, the Creator, the Redeemer, the King. He is in control. Then look away from character development to Christ. Only by beholding Him—not self—will you become changed into His likeness.

Just as it is imperative to shift your concern away from your personal deliverance to the Deliverer who alone can bring salvation, so you must look away from the delay in the Advent to the Advent itself. Christ is coming—He is in control. Even though Satan works with frenzy to manipulate mankind through TV, the occult, the charismatic movement, and spiritualism, Christ's return overthrows all his efforts. They are but wild jabs in the dark which have time against them.

The greatest proof that God is in charge is the

FINAL EVENTS ON PLANET EARTH

fact that He will have the last word. We must study human history in the light of its final event. God has the last move. Like moves on a chessboard, the plays and counterplays lead inevitably to His checkmate—to Christ's return as King of kings and Lord of lords.

More important than *what* is coming is *who* is coming. And who is He? God is great! Take the universe He created, for instance. The October, 1974, *Reader's Digest* reports on "the fantastic world of outer space."[13] If the thickness of a page of this book represented the distance from earth to the sun (93 million miles) then the span to the nearest star is a 71-foot-high sheaf of paper. The diameter of our own galaxy is a 310-mile-high stack of paper, and the edge of the known universe is an astonishing pile thirty-one million miles high.

Our world is in the Milky Way Galaxy. Scientists estimate that perhaps 100 billion galaxies exist in the universe. Truly "this world is but an atom in the vast dominions over which God presides, yet this little fallen world—the one lost sheep—is more precious in His sight than are the ninety and nine that went not astray from the fold."[14] What a condescension for the omnipresent Christ to come to our little world to become but one man. And the God-man would have gone through all His infinite humiliation just for one person— just for you. "Jesus cares for each one as though there were not another individual on the face of the earth."[15] Our hearts cry out, "How great Thou art!"

The fact of Christ's incarnation is the guarantee

WHAT'S COMING?

of His devotion to you. His perfect human life is your robe of righteousness. His death assures His forgiveness for you. His resurrection provides the certainty that He lives for you, and the fact of His coming advent promises you that you have an eternal future. He, Jesus Christ, is the greatest fact that God is in control of His universe, despite all puzzling circumstances to the contrary.

The church can rest assured and secure in His benevolent control which brings freedom.

---

[1] Ellen G. White, *Sons and Daughters of God* (Washington, D.C.: Review and Herald Publishing Association, 1955), p. 168.

[2] Ellen G. White, *The Ministry of Healing* (Mountain View, California: Pacific Press Publishing Association, 1942), p. 241.

[3] *Testimonies for the Church,* Vol. 5, p. 315.

[4] Ellen G. White, Letter 115, 1904, in *The Seventh-day Adventist Bible Commentary* (Washington, D.C.: Review and Herald Publishing Association, 1956), Vol. 5, p. 1110.

[5] *Testimonies for the Church,* Vol. 2, p. 604.

[6] Ellen G. White, *Steps to Christ* (Washington, D.C.: Review and Herald Publishing Association, 1908), p. 71.

[7] Ellen G. White, *Prophets and Kings* (Mountain View: Pacific Press Publishing Association, 1917), p. 162, emphasis supplied.

[8] *Patriarchs and Prophets,* p. 482.

[9] *The Desire of Ages,* p. 216.

[10] Ellen G. White, *The Acts of the Apostles* (Mountain View, California: Pacific Press Publishing Association, 1911), p. 325.

[11] *Testimonies to Ministers and Gospel Workers,* pp. 473, 474.

[12] *Early Writings,* p. 58.

[13] *Reader's Digest,* (Asian edition), "The Fantastic World of Outer Space," by Kenneth F. Weaver, October, 1974, pp. 65-72.

[14] Ellen G. White, *Christ's Object Lessons* (Washington, D.C.: Review and Herald Publishing Association, 1941), p. 190.

[15] *Testimonies for the Church,* Vol. 5, p. 346.

FINAL EVENTS ON PLANET EARTH